PRENTICE HALL
BOOK DISTRIBUTION CENTER
Route 59 at Brook Hill Drive
West Nyack, New York 10995

PLACE
STAMP
HERE

PRENTICE HALL
BOOK DISTRIBUTION CENTER
Route 59 at Brook Hill Drive
West Nyack, New York 10995

Please send me a copy of the cassette tape listed below:

☐ One 90-minute cassette to accompany PROFESSIONAL INTERACTIONS: ORAL COMMUNICATION SKILLS IN SCIENCE, TECHNOLOGY, AND MEDICINE (Matthews/Marino), 72609-1, $15.00 (Price may vary outside the United States and is subject to change without notice.)

Name _____

Address _____

City _____ State _____ Zip _____

Indicate form of payment:

☐ check or money order payable to Prentice Hall. Write the check for the amount listed above plus your state's sales tax. (If you pay by check or money order, Prentice Hall will pay for shipping and handling.)

☐ Visa   ☐ Mastercard

Expiration date _____

Account number _____

Signature _____

For international orders, please contact your local Prentice Hall office.

Please send me a copy of the cassette tape listed below:

☐ One 90-minute cassette to accompany PROFESSIONAL INTERACTIONS: ORAL COMMUNICATION SKILLS IN SCIENCE, TECHNOLOGY, AND MEDICINE (Matthews/Marino), 72609-1, $15.00 (Price may vary outside the United States and is subject to change without notice.)

Name _____

Address _____

City _____ State _____ Zip _____

Indicate form of payment:

☐ check or money order payable to Prentice Hall. Write the check for the amount listed above plus your state's sales tax. (If you pay by check or money order, Prentice Hall will pay for shipping and handling.)

☐ Visa   ☐ Mastercard

Expiration date _____

Account number _____

Signature _____

For international orders, please contact your local Prentice Hall office.

*Oral Communication Skills
in Science, Technology, and Medicine*

Professional Interactions

Candace Matthews
*Institute of North American Studies
Barcelona, Spain*

Joanne Marino
Kuwait University

Drawings by Paul Docksey

Prentice Hall Regents
Englewood Cliffs, New Jersey 07632

Library of Congress Cataloging-in-Publication Data

Matthews, Candace
    Professional interactions: oral communication skills in science,
technology, and medicine / Candace Matthews, Joanne Marino;
drawings by Paul Docksey.
        p. cm.
    ISBN 0–13–726084–9
    1. Communication in science. 2. Communication of technical
information. 3. Communication in medicine. 4. Oral communication.
I. Marino, Joanne. II. Title.
    [DNLM: 1. Communication. 2. Interpersonal Relations. 3. Speech.
BF 637.C45 M438p]
Q224.M38 1990
501.4—dc20
DGPO/DLC
for Library of Congress   89–26440
                                                                      CIP

Editorial/production supervision: Lynn Alden Kendall
Interior design: Karen Buck
Cover design: Wanda Lubelska Design
Manufacturing buyer: Raymond Keating

 © 1990 by Prentice-Hall, Inc.
A Division of Simon & Schuster
Englewood Cliffs, New Jersey 07632

Portions of this book have appeared in slightly different form in
Candace Matthews, *Business Interactions* (Englewood Cliffs, N.J.:
Prentice Hall, 1986).

Printed in the United States of America
10 9 8 7 6 5 4 3 2 1

ISBN 0-13-726084-9

Prentice-Hall International (UK) Limited, *London*
Prentice-Hall of Australia Pty. Limited, *Sydney*
Prentice-Hall Canada Inc., *Toronto*
Prentice-Hall Hispanoamericana, S.A., *Mexico*
Prentice-Hall of India Private Limited, *New Delhi*
Prentice-Hall of Japan, Inc., *Tokyo*
Simon & Schuster Asia Pte. Ltd., *Singapore*
Editora Prentice-Hall do Brasil, Ltda., *Rio de Janeiro*

Photo credits: *Page 17: top left,* General Electric Research and Development Center; *top right,* Air France; *middle left,* On-Line Software International; *bottom left,* Cecil Yarbrough; *bottom right,* South African Consulate General Information Section, New York. *Page 75: top left,* U.S. Coast Guard; *top right,* American Red Cross; *bottom left,* UNICEF Photo by Steiner; *bottom right,* Ken Karp. *Page 121: top left,* Marc Anderson; *top right,* Eugene Gordon; *bottom left,* UNICEF Photo by John Weisblat; *bottom right,* Eastman Kodak Company. *Page 137: top left,* Commonwealth Edison Company; *top right,* United Nations; *bottom left,* Irene Springer; *bottom right,* National Highway Traffic Safety Administration. *Page 182: top left,* Chrysler Corporation; *top right,* Aluminum Company of America; *bottom left,* United Nations/B. Zarov/MOJ; *bottom right,* Bureau of Reclamation, Department of the Interior. *Page 228: top left,* WHO Photo by P. Almasy; *top right,* United Nations; *bottom left and right,* United Nations/B. Wolff.

Contents

iii

UNIT 3   Handling Suggestions

UNIT 9   Analyzing Solutions 1
Group Discussion Skills   **132**

UNIT 13   Using Visual Aids
Oral Presentation Skills   *191*

UNIT 14   Comparing
Group Discussion Skills   *207*

UNIT 15　Persuading
Group Discussion Skills　223

Appendices

Contents Overview

Oral Presentation Skills

Group Discussion Skills

	Expressions	*Communication Concepts*	*Discussion Techniques*	*Discussion Practice*
Unit 2	Giving an opinion Agreeing Disagreeing Asking about agreement	Language styles	Introducing a discussion	Solving a problem
Unit 3	Making a suggestion Accepting a suggestion Rejecting a suggestion Showing doubt	Effective meetings	Closing a discussion	Solving a problem
Unit 5	Asking for information Asking about support Supporting an idea Opposing an idea	Effective leadership	Keeping communication open	Analyzing a problem
Unit 6	Stating a fact Refuting Asking for examples Giving examples	Effective participation	Interrupting	Solving a problem
Unit 8	Asking for clarification Clarifying Paraphrasing Asking for further information	Steps in problem solving	Getting a point into the discussion	Ranking in order
Unit 9	Asking about cost Analyzing cost Asking about time Analyzing time Asking about side effects Analyzing side effects	Effective listening	Avoiding answering	Solving a problem

	Expressions	*Communication Concepts*	*Discussion Techniques*	*Discussion Practice*
Unit 11	Asking about feasibility Analyzing feasibility Asking about acceptability Analyzing acceptability Asking about effectiveness Analyzing effectiveness	Group task roles	Correcting yourself	Solving a problem
Unit 12	Asking about possible consequences Predicting possible consequences Asking about alternatives Expressing possibility	Group building roles	Keeping the discussion moving	Solving a problem
Unit 14	Asking about priorities Stating priorities Comparing two solutions Comparing three or more solutions Expressing similarities	Individual blocking roles	Returning to the subject	Determining criteria
Unit 15	Persuading Counterarguing Conceding	Nonverbal communication	Summarizing	Solving a problem

Preface

PURPOSE

The purpose of *Professional Interactions* is to develop the oral communication skills of EFL/ESL students working as professionals in science, engineering, medicine, or related fields. Functional in approach, the text focuses on two vital areas of professional communication: giving presentations and taking part in meetings or small group discussions. The subject matter, drawn from various technical fields, is provocative and timely but never too specialized.

Ten units of the text (Units 2, 3, 5, 6, 8, 9, 11, 12, 14, 15) are devoted to training students in the skills of small group interaction. As students are guided through the process of interacting effectively, they are able to develop communicative strategies that carry over into real-life situations. Providing essential practice in controlled exercises followed by opportunities for expansion in freer communicative activities, the text enables students to focus on forms, functions, and the processes of oral discourse. Emphasizing student-student interaction, these units are designed to help students:

- become familiar with various expressions related to specific language functions
- improve listening skills by focusing on both content and the use of these expressions in task-based listening exercises based on a cassette featuring both American and British native speakers
- build up speaking skills by practicing functional expressions and focusing on grammar, vocabulary, and pronunciation in controlled practice exercises

- learn or review basic subtechnical vocabulary
- apply the principles of group interaction as active participants and leaders in problem-solving discussions based on scientific, technical, and medical situations
- analyze group interaction and individual/group effectiveness through the use of a variety of carefully designed evaluation forms

The units dealing with oral presentation skills are integrated within the text (Units 1, 4, 7, 10, 13). With this integration, the text provides opportunities for review and expansion of the skills throughout the term. Furthermore, this method of organization allows the class to alternate between group work and individual presentations, thus providing an interesting change of pace for the students and instructor. The five units are designed to help students:

- plan, organize, develop, and deliver presentations by following clear, step-by-step guidelines
- build up self-confidence through practicing isolated presentation skills (such as introducing/closing a presentation, using transitions, and handling questions) in small groups
- gain experience in giving different types of presentations on suggested or student-chosen topics
- practice careful, focused listening through completing a variety of listening assignments based on in-class presentations
- learn how to analyze the effectiveness of presentations by using evaluation forms that gradually increase in complexity as students progress through the course

The abundance of material in the text makes it easily adaptable to varying learner interests, student specialties, class sizes, and language levels. The students and/or instructor can select the exercises, topics, and activities that are most relevant to the needs of the class.

TYPES OF STUDENTS

Professional Interactions is designed for science, engineering, or health professionals at an intermediate to advanced level of English proficiency. The text is appropriate for professionals working in industry, medical facilities, academic institutions, or international organizations who want to learn how to communicate effectively in English.

The book is also intended for undergraduate or graduate students preparing for careers in these fields who need to improve their speaking skills.

COMPONENTS

The complete course consists of:

- This book
- Instructor's Manual
- Cassette

Acknowledgments

This book would not have been possible without the generous help and support of many friends and colleagues. In particular, we would like to express our sincere gratitude to the following people for their special efforts: the teachers of the Medical and Study Skills Division of Kuwait University for piloting much of the material and providing useful feedback; Barbara Hayward, for carefully reviewing the manuscript and offering many valuable suggestions, especially on the listening scripts; Philip Reavey and Peter Holliday, for their technical advice; Dan Byra, Diane Pinkley, and James Purpura, for their helpful suggestions and input; Michael Compton, for his special help and support; David Haines for his invaluable assistance in the production of the audio cassette; Isobel Fletcher de Tellaz, for supervising the recording of the audio cassette; Anne Riddick, for her help with the project; and Lynn Kendall, for supervising the production of the book.

We would like to dedicate this book to our families.

Introduction:
To the Student

This book is designed to help you improve your speaking skills in two important areas of professional communication: taking part in meetings or small group discussions and giving presentations. Ten units of the book deal with small group discussion skills. As you work through these units, you will learn how to take part effectively in discussions in English. These units (Units 2, 3, 5, 6, 8, 9, 11, 12, 14, and 15) generally consist of the following sections:

Expressions

This section contains lists of some expressions that are commonly used to convey different language functions, such as agreeing, disagreeing, suggesting, and asking for further information. The expressions listed in each unit are limited to those that are most commonly used in professional situations. Since not all possible expressions are listed, you may want to add to the lists as you work through the unit.

Listening Practice

These exercises, based on an accompanying audio cassette with both American and British speakers, are designed to give you practice in comprehending dialogs and discussions on topics related to science, technology, and medicine. You may listen to each exercise several times, focusing first on content and then on language use. In this way you can work on understanding what the speakers say as well as how they say it. Furthermore, you will become familiar with the way speakers use the expressions in a variety of realistic contexts.

Controlled Practice

This section contains a number of different exercises designed to give you practice in using the expressions in a controlled context. Through this controlled practice, you should be able to remember the expressions more easily and be able to use them correctly and appropriately. Since these exercises cover topics in science, engineering, and medicine, your instructor can select those items that are most appropriate for the students in your class.

The purpose of this controlled practice is for you to become familiar with different expressions so that you can add variety to your language. The more expressions that you are able to use, the more effective you can be as a speaker. Furthermore, these exercises will give you a chance to work on improving your control of grammar, building your vocabulary, or refining your pronunciation.

Communication Concepts

The guidelines and principles explained in this section are included to help you gain a better understanding of the processes involved in small group interaction.

Discussion Techniques

This section includes brief explanations of some of the special techniques used in small group discussions that you can practice in the small group activities included in the following section of the text.

Discussion Practice

This section contains different types of group activities intended to stimulate discussion. The different types of activities include problem solving, problem analysis, ranking of priorities, and determining criteria. The subject matter is drawn from the fields of science, engineering, and health, so the instructor or class members can choose the activities that are the most interesting to the students in your class. This means that your class may not cover all of the activities in this section—just the ones that are the most useful or appropriate.

Early units provide you with detailed guidance in preparing for each discussion. This preparation is very important because it helps you develop useful ideas to contribute to the discussion. Once you know what you want to say, you can work on communicating those ideas clearly to the others in your group. You can then follow these same steps in preparing for later group discussions.

The group activities in this section give you a chance to practice the skills that have been presented in the unit. It is important to have a class atmosphere in which everyone feels comfortable about taking part in the group activities, because you can improve your speaking ability only through practice. Also, you should not worry about making mistakes; they are a natural and expected part of learning another language. The key to success is to be able to learn from the mistakes that you and others make.

Discussion Evaluation

A variety of observer evaluation forms are included to help you learn how to analyze the performance of other groups and other students. With these evaluation forms, observers can learn how to offer helpful suggestions, while participants receive useful feedback. Another type of participant evaluation form is designed to help you analyze the interaction and effectiveness of your own group. Finally, three self-evaluation forms are included to help you become aware of your own strengths and weaknesses. All of these different forms include specific points to help you understand the dynamics of group interaction.

It is important for you to be open to both giving and receiving suggestions on how to improve the discussions. Learning to speak is not a competition. It is a group effort. You are all working toward the same goal: learning how to speak effectively in a group discussion. You will find that you can learn as much from your failures as from your successes.

Units 1, 4, 7, 10, and 13 deal with giving presentations. These units generally consist of the following sections:

Presentation Preparation	This section includes guidelines covering different aspects of preparing a presentation. A number of pair or small group activities are included in this section to help you build up your presentation skills gradually.
Presentation Techniques	This section provides you with clear guidelines of basic presentation techniques, followed by small group activities to give you practice in applying the techniques.
Presentation Assignments	Each unit includes a list of different types of presentations in addition to specific examples of possible topics. These assignments are intended as suggestions of the many types of presentations that are possible. The instructor will decide whether to assign you a specific type of presentation from the list, choose another topic, or allow you to choose your own topic.
Suggested Assignments for Listeners	Each unit contains suggested activities for listeners in order to focus their attention on the presentations given by students in the class. The instructor may give you all the same assignment or may choose different assignments for students in the class.
Presentation Evaluation	The evaluation forms for each unit are based on the specific skills presented in the unit. In addition, the form for each unit includes the skills presented in the previous units. In this way, the forms build up in complexity as you progress through the course. These evaluation forms will help you learn how to analyze the effectiveness of other presentations.

Developing a Delivery Style

Professionals in science, engineering, or medicine are often asked to provide people with information because they have specialized knowledge or experience. Technical professionals may be called on to give progress reports, explain research, discuss company policies, analyze problems, offer recommendations, or give on-the-job instructions. In addition, they may give oral presentations to accompany more formal written reports, such as project proposals, budget proposals, or feasibility studies.

As a professional in science, your primary interest and training may be in technical areas. Nevertheless, you need to develop effective communication skills so that you can clearly convey your ideas and information to other people. You may have to speak to colleagues, patients, technicians, managers, contractors, consultants, salespeople, or visiting lecturers. You may find yourself speaking at an informal gathering or giving a formal presentation at a conference, talking to experts or nonexperts. In all cases you will need to be able to present your information in a clear, well-organized manner. The five units in this book on oral presentation skills (Units 1, 4, 7, 10, 13) will help you learn how to plan, organize, and present information on a variety of topics. The experience you gain in preparing and giving in-class presentations should give you the necessary skills to face any future speaking situation with confidence.

ACTIVITY 1-A

1. Work in small groups. Make a list of all the different types of speaking situations, such as giving progress reports or speaking at conferences, that members in your group have faced. Include the situations in which you spoke your native language as well as those in which you spoke English.
2. Put a check mark next to the situations in which some or any of you had to use English. Discuss any difficulties you had in using English in these situations.
3. If people in your group used English in only a few situations, make a list of your reasons for studying English.
4. When all the groups have finished, compare your lists.

Presentation Preparation

DEVELOPING A STYLE OF DELIVERY

Delivery refers to the way you use your eyes, voice, and body to communicate your message. Of course, what you say is important, but the way you say it also has a strong effect on your listeners.

A. Styles of Delivery

When you speak to a group of people, you should choose the most appropriate style of delivery for your message, your listeners, and your speaking situation. A presentation may be extemporaneous, impromptu, memorized, or read from a manuscript.

An *extemporaneous* delivery is carefully prepared and practiced in advance. Since this is the most effective way of speaking to a group, it is the style of delivery that you will practice in this course. When preparing an extemporaneous presentation, you have the time to gather the information, outline your ideas, plan the introduction and conclusion, prepare notes, and practice the presentation before you give it. You can use note cards with an outline of the main ideas to help remind you of the order of the ideas that you want to present. With this style of delivery, your ideas are thought out in advance, but you do not memorize the exact wording of your presentation. You speak in a natural, conversational style with only quick glances at your notes when necessary.

An *impromptu* presentation is made with little or no advance planning. For example, you might have to make an impromptu presentation at work if you are asked without warning to explain to several people how your department functions, how a particular machine works, or why a certain project has been delayed. Clearly, it is difficult to be well-organized and effective without advance preparation. However, the experience you gain in organizing and presenting your ideas in extemporaneous presentations can help you improve your effectiveness in impromptu speaking situations.

A *memorized* presentation is one that you write out completely in advance and then learn word for word. Although a memorized presentation allows you to look at the listeners as you are speaking, you often have to concentrate more on remembering the report than on communicating the information. You may find it difficult to sound natural when you are trying to recite from memory. Also, you are always faced with the possibility of forgetting what comes next. For these reasons, you should not try to memorize your presentations for this course.

A *manuscript* presentation is written out in full and then read aloud to the listeners. This type of presentation may be given in a very formal situation, such as at an academic or professional conference, when the message is extremely complex or technical. Although you may feel more secure reading a report, you will discover how difficult it is to keep your audience's attention, to sound natural, and to adapt your presentation to suit the listeners' reactions when you are reading aloud. Because of the many disadvantages of reading a report aloud, you will not practice this type of delivery in this course.

B. Effective Delivery

By showing enthusiasm for your subject, you can make your listeners more interested in what you have to say. You can make your presentation more effective by considering how you use your eyes, voice, and body when you are speaking to a group of people.

Eye contact is essential in keeping your listeners' interest. Of course, you can glance at your notes occasionally, but people are more likely to pay attention if you look at their faces directly as you are speaking. By moving your eyes from person to person, you can give listeners the feeling that you are talking to them as individuals. You can also see whether or not people are following your message by watching their faces.

Your *voice* also plays an important role in keeping your listeners' attention. Obviously, it is impossible to keep people's interest if they cannot hear what you are saying. Furthermore, you must pronounce your words clearly and distinctly, speaking at a normal rate of speed, so that people can easily understand you. By speaking in a natural, conversational manner, you will help people in a group feel that you are talking to them as individuals rather than giving a prepared speech.

Finally, the way you use your *body* conveys a message to your listeners. You can show people that you are confident by standing or sitting up straight and not leaning against a table or a desk. Hand or arm gestures can be effective if you feel natural and comfortable using them. In general, though, you do not want to distract listeners from your message by playing with a pencil, shifting from one foot to the other, or doing anything else to draw attention to yourself.

ACTIVITY 1-B

1. Work in small groups. Based on personal experience and the information presented in this unit, make a list of specific guidelines that speakers should follow in making presentations. For example: "Speakers should talk loudly enough so that everyone can hear them."
2. When all the groups have finished, compare your lists.
3. You may want to make a master list of guidelines for students to follow in giving presentations in class. If possible, the instructor can make photocopies for everyone in the class.

ACTIVITY 1-C

1. Prepare a two- to three-minute presentation about something that happened to you. The story may be about a funny, exciting, or frightening experience, such as an accident or a trip.
2. Now work in small groups. Take turns presenting your stories to the group. After each presentation, discuss the strengths and weaknesses of the speaker's delivery style. How can the speaker improve his or her delivery style in future presentations?

ACTIVITY 1-D

1. Work with a partner. If possible, choose someone you don't know, who speaks a different native language. Spend ten to twelve minutes interviewing each other.
2. The instructor will then call on pairs of students to introduce each other to the rest of the class. Use details in your introduction to make your partner memorable and interesting to the other students.
3. In interviewing and introducing your partner, you may include some or all of the following information, depending on whether he or she is currently employed or is a full-time student:
   - name (perhaps written on the board)
   - nationality
   - current occupation or occupation planned after graduation
   - place of work/position or title of job
   - major duties and responsibilities of job
   - past work experience
   - reasons for interest in this field
   - educational background
   - major field of study/specialization
   - special areas of interest/research in this field
   - hobbies or special interests
   - past English study (where and how long)
   - need for English
   - reasons for taking this particular course
4. When everyone has finished, decide which introduction was the most interesting or the most memorable.

Presentation Techniques

INTRODUCING A PRESENTATION

The purpose of an introduction is to attract your listeners' interest and focus their attention on your topic. When you give a presentation at work, your listeners usually have an immediate need for the information you are presenting. Therefore, they have a clear reason to pay attention to your presentation. Still, you should try to increase their natural interest in the subject by emphasizing how useful or how important the information is. Listeners generally pay closer attention to a presentation if they know in advance how they can benefit from the information.

Another important function of the introduction is to identify what your presentation is about and how you plan to present the information. For example, you may tell the listeners that you are first going to explain a particular problem, then briefly mention some of its causes, and finally focus on several possible solutions. This brief preview of the content and organization of your presentation allows the listeners to fit the information you give them into a framework and helps them understand and remember what you present. A final point to mention in the introduction is whether listeners are free to interrupt you with questions or whether they should save their questions for the end of the presentation. If you plan to allow time at the end for a question-and-answer session, you should inform your listeners at the beginning of the presentation.

Because presentations given at work often differ from those given in class, you may find that the introductions are also different. In a classroom situation your listeners do not always have a natural interest in what you want to say to them. Therefore, you may have to work harder to get the attention of your audience. You have to plan a strong introduction in order to make people want to hear the rest of your presentation. The best way to interest your listeners is to relate your topic to their wants and needs. Listeners usually pay close attention to what affects them directly: their work, their interests, their health, their security, their family, their friends, or their community. Furthermore, most listeners have a natural curiosity to learn more about the world. You can try to appeal to this curiosity in your introduction. Certain types of openings are often effective in gaining an audience's attention. You might start with one of the following:

- a surprising or unusual fact
- a personal story
- an interesting example
- a quotation from an authority or expert
- impressive or significant statistics

Of course, any opening that you use should relate directly to your topic, or it will only confuse the listeners.

An effective introduction to any type of presentation should be brief and to the point. You want to capture the interest of your listeners and then lead them into the content of your presentation. You should never use the introduction to apologize to the audience for anything: for being nervous, for not being prepared, for not being an expert on the subject. By taking a positive, confident approach from the beginning of your presentation, you will make the listeners eager to hear what you have to say on the subject.

ACTIVITY 1-E

1. Choose a problem in class, at work, in the community, or in the country where you live. Examples of such problems include drug abuse, local pollution, or poor library facilities. Select a problem that you feel deserves the special attention of the students in your class.
2. Work individually to prepare a one- to two-minute introduction to a presentation on the topic. Develop an effective introduction that you feel will attract the listeners' interest and focus their attention on the topic.
3. When everyone has finished, work in small groups. Take turns presenting your introductions to the group. After each speaker has finished, discuss the strengths and weaknesses of the introduction. Did the speaker include all of the elements of an effective introduction?

Presentation Assignment 1

After studying the information in this unit, you can prepare a three- to five-minute presentation to give to a group or to the entire class. Look at the presentation evaluation form on page 10 to see how you will be evaluated. Your instructor may assign a topic or allow you to choose your own. Before giving your presentation, you should practice it several times. Practice will give you a chance to think about, evaluate, and revise your presentation. It will also give you greater self-confidence and help you feel more relaxed. Here are some guidelines to follow when practicing your presentation.

1. Practice your presentation in front of your family or friends. Ask them for their honest opinions.
2. Go through the entire presentation when you practice it even if you have difficulty in a particular place. Notice the rough spots so you can work on them before you practice the presentation again.
3. Practice the presentation enough so that you know the information very well. However, do not try to memorize the exact words that you will use.
4. Use your notes when you practice the presentation. Be sure to use the same note cards in practice as you plan to use in giving the presentation. You should be familiar with those particular notes when you give the report.
5. Time your presentation in practice to make sure that it meets the time requirements. Keep in mind that when you give the actual

presentation you may talk a bit more rapidly or forget some details due to nervousness. Therefore, make sure that your presentation is long enough.
6. If possible, tape-record or videotape your practice. By watching or listening to yourself, you may be able to see more clearly how to improve your presentation.
7. As you practice, think about the parts of your presentation that might bring questions from the listeners. Be prepared to support your ideas and give the sources of your information.

Suggested Topics

1. Imagine that you are speaking to a group of consultants who are evaluating the efficiency of your department. Give a detailed description of the duties and responsibilities of your present job.
2. Imagine that you are speaking to some students who are interested in majoring in your particular field of study. Discuss the different job opportunities in this field.
3. Discuss a recent development or innovation in your field.
   Guidelines:
   The presentation should include:
   • how it was developed
   • current and future applications or uses
   • what needs the development meets
   • any problems associated with it
4. Discuss a research project that you have carried out.
   Guidelines:
   The presentation should include:
   • the purpose of the research
   • what you did
   • when and where you carried out the research
   • significant results/conclusions/recommendations
5. Discuss the significant contributions of a scientist in your field. You might choose a scientist who is not familiar to the students in your class.
   Sample scientists:
   James Clerk Maxwell
   Abdellah Avicenna (also spelled Ibn Sina)
   Antoine Becquerel
   Helen Taussig

Robert Hooke
Al-Khwarizmi
Hideyo Noguchi
Christiaan Eijkman
Hans Oersted
Rachel Carson

6. Choose a recent Nobel Prize winner in your area of specialization. Explain the significance of that person's contribution.

Suggested Assignments for Listeners

The instructor may assign different students to do some of the following listening assignments. The listeners should then turn in their assignments to the instructor, give them to the speaker, or discuss their results with the rest of the group or class, according to the teacher's instructions.

1. Fill out the evaluation form.
2. Write two questions to ask the speaker after the presentation.
3. Pay particular attention to the introduction. Consider the following questions in analyzing the strengths and weaknesses of the introduction:
   A. How did the speaker gain attention?
   B. What was the central idea of the presentation? Was it clearly stated?
   C. What preview did the speaker give of the organization of the presentation?
   D. How did the speaker plan to handle questions from the audience?
   E. Can you offer any suggestions for improving the introduction?
4. Be prepared to answer any questions about the presentation that your instructor may ask you.

Presentation Evaluation 1

Speaker: _____

Topic: _____

Evaluator: _____

Rating System
Complete the following evaluation form by filling in the appropriate number of points in the blanks provided. The point values are as follows:

2 = Excellent   1 = Satisfactory   0 = Needs Improvement

These points can be added up to give a total score for this section. Other sections will be added to the evaluation forms in future presentation units. Space is provided on the form for your comments on specific strengths or weaknesses of the speaker's presentation. You can also add suggestions for improving future presentations.

I. *Delivery*

Points out of 10: _____   *Comments:*

_____ A. volume—loud enough
         to be heard clearly
_____ B. eye contact with audi-
         ence
_____ C. natural delivery—not
         read or memorized
_____ D. rate of speech—not too
         fast or too slow
_____ E. posture/body move-
         ment—no distracting
         mannerisms

Total Number of Points Received by Speaker: _____

Total Number of Possible Points: _____

Questions to ask the speaker:

1. _____

2. _____

Exchanging Opinions

Expressions

In a group discussion, speakers use a wide variety of language functions, such as giving opinions, making statements, agreeing, disagreeing, suggesting, persuading, and many others. Speakers may directly signal these language functions through the use of certain phrases or expressions in English, or they may convey them indirectly without using any particular expressions.

The main advantage of using set expressions is that they help to make a speaker's intentions clear. For example, the expression, "I see what you mean, but . . ." signals that the speaker is going to disagree with the preceding comment. By using such expressions, a speaker helps the listeners understand the purpose of a particular comment or question and see how it relates to the ideas previously expressed. With ideas more clearly connected, listeners usually find it easier to follow the flow of the discussion and respond appropriately. In this way, the use of expressions helps reduce confusion and leads to clearer communication in a group.

Many different expressions, of course, can be used to convey each function in English. These expressions are not necessarily interchangeable, however; some may be more formal or informal, more direct or indirect, than others. The expressions listed in this section are limited to some examples that are generally appropriate in professional situations. This list of expressions is intended to be a reference source that you can add to as you work through the unit.

Before going over the lists provided, you may want to discuss each function and then work individually or in small groups to list expressions you are already familiar with. You can identify any expressions that seem to be particularly formal, informal, direct, or indirect and then compare them with those listed here. You might also discuss possible situations in which these expressions could appropriately be used.

Giving an opinion
I think _____.
I believe _____.
In my opinion, _____.
As far as I'm concerned, _____.
As I see it, _____.
Personally, I think _____.
It seems to me _____.

Asking about agreement
Do you agree?
Don't you agree?
Wouldn't you agree?
Don't you think so?

Agreeing
That's right.   I agree with you.
You're right.   I definitely agree.
I think so, too.   I completely agree with you.
That's a good point.   I couldn't agree with you more.

Disagreeing
I don't think so.
That's not how I see it.
I don't really agree with you.
I'm afraid I can't agree with you.
I'm not sure I quite agree with you.
Yes, that may be true, but _____.
Well, you have a point there, but _____.
I can see your point, but _____.
I see what you mean, but _____.

Listening Practice

The following exercises can be completed by listening to Unit 2 on the tape.

Section 1. There are eight separate dialogs in this section. All of these dialogs are about the same general subject. A laboratory experiment has been repeated by another research team. However, the research team did not get the expected results.

A. Listen to Section 1 on the tape. For each dialog complete the statement concerning what the first speaker said. Circle the letter of the correct answer.

1. The man thinks that the new technician was ___B___.
    a. careful   b. careless

2. The woman believes that the instruments were _____.
    a. dirty   b. clean

3. The man believes that the data were recorded ___B___.
    a. correctly   b. incorrectly

4. The woman wants the _____ adjusted.
    a. scale   b. weights

5. The man believes that the experimental team _____ follow the instructions.
    a. did   b. did not

6. The woman thinks that the _____ made a mistake.
    a. technician   b. typist

7. The man thinks that the original experimental group reported the experiment ___B___.
    a. falsely   b. truthfully

8. The woman believes that the results differed from the original results because the ___B___ was wrong.
    a. cylinder   b. measurement

B. Work with a partner, in a small group, or as a class to compare your answers.

C. Listen again. This time decide whether the second speaker agrees or disagrees with the first. Put a check [✔] in the correct space.

	Agree	Disagree	Expressions *"I can't agree with you"*
1.	✗	X	*She is responble for it*
2.	X		*use the equip for a month*
3.		X	*double check*
4.	✗	X	*more serious problem*
5.	X		*didn't plan anything*
6.		X	*secretary very careful*
7.	✗		*excellent reputation*
8.	X		*that a good point*

D. Listen a third time. Write the expression that the second speaker uses to agree or disagree.

E. Work with a partner, in a small group, or as a class to compare your answers.

Section 2. There is one discussion in this section. Three people are discussing a government plan to reduce the level of lead in the atmosphere by limiting the use of leaded gasoline.

A. Look at the following points. Which of these points do the speakers mention? Listen to Section 2 on the tape. Put a check [✓] next to the ideas that are mentioned in the discussion.

_✗_ 1. It's difficult for the car industry to make quick changes in production.

_____ 2. Older cars need lead to run efficiently.

_✗_ 3. Leaded fumes harm young children.

_____ 4. Catalytic converters reduce exhaust pollution.

_✗_ 5. Any engine can be designed to run well on unleaded gas.

_✗_ 6. The government should lower the tax on unleaded gas.

B. Listen again. What expressions do the speakers use to introduce their opinions? Make a list of these expressions in the order that you hear them.

Expressions

1. _____ goverment plan a good idea _____
2. _____ Well I think _____
3. _____ personal I think _____
4. _____ I believe _____
5. _____ it seem to me _____
6. _____ I concern _____

C. Work with a partner, in a small group, or as a class to compare your answers in Parts A and B.

Controlled Practice

This section contains exercises to give you practice in using various expressions from the unit. The purpose here is for you to gain control of some different expressions so that you can accurately and appropriately use them in group discussions. These exercises also give you a chance to work on improving your control of grammar, building up your vocabulary, and refining your pronunciation in order to communicate your ideas as clearly as possible. You do not need to cover every item or exercise in this section, but your instructor will give you as much practice as you need to feel comfortable using these expressions.

Exercise 1.   Use different expressions from the unit in discussing the illustrations on page 17.

> *Speaker A:*   Give your opinion.
>
> *Speaker B:*   Agree or disagree.

Exercise 2.   Use different expressions from the unit.

> *Speaker A:*   Give an opinion on the topic. Then ask about agreement or disagreement.
>
> *Speaker B:*   Agree or disagree.

1. the best _____
   A. season of the year
   B. brand of stereo to buy
   C. foreign language to learn

   D. conductor of heat
   E. physical exercise
   F. source of vitamin C

2. the worst _____
   A. kind of natural disaster
   B. car to drive
   C. airline to fly
   D. day of the week
   E. building material for a house
   F. country for a vacation

3. the most _____
   A. useful piece of laboratory equipment
   B. difficult science subject
   C. serious problem in the world
   D. useful alloy
   E. significant invention in history
   F. important duty of a nurse

4. the best way to _____
   A. preserve the world's wildlife
   B. encourage scientific research
   C. treat the common cold
   D. stop water pollution
   E. reduce the number of deaths from cancer
   F. stay healthy

Exercise 3.   Use different expressions from the unit.

   Speaker A: Give an opinion on the topic. Then ask about
                  agreement or disagreement.
   Speaker B: Agree or disagree.

1. the best system of measurement
2. the best way to treat a fever
3. the greatest scientific discovery
4. the most serious environmental problem
5. the best way to avoid tooth decay
6. the most interesting scientific department to work in
7. the best computer game to play
8. the safest means of transportation
9. the most important use of lasers
10. the best way to dispose of industrial waste
11. the most important use of nuclear energy
12. the best way to prevent air pollution

1. electric cars

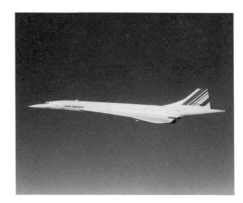

2. supersonic aircraft

3. portable computers

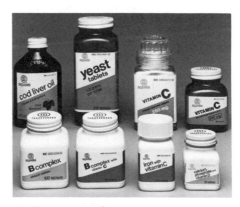

4. dietary supplements

5. crash diets

6. big cities

13. the best way to relax
14. the most important use of satellites
15. the best way to prevent drug addiction
16. the most efficient kind of engine
17. the most needed skill in engineering
18. the most useful synthetic material
19. the most difficult medical specialty
20. the most important quality of a health professional

Communication Concepts

LANGUAGE STYLES

Speakers of English can use different styles of language to communicate the same idea. For example, you may choose a formal or an informal style of saying the same thing:

Informal	Formal
Thanks.	Thank you very much.
Hi.	Good afternoon.
Sit down.	Would you care to sit down?
Can you give me a hand?	I'd certainly appreciate it if you could help me.
Great idea!	In my opinion, that is an excellent suggestion.

In most situations a neutral style of language (between formal and informal) is acceptable. However, a special situation may require you to use a more formal or informal style.

Discuss how each of the following factors might influence your choice of formal or informal English:

1. What is your relationship to the other speaker?
   - relative
   - friend
   - acquaintance
   - stranger
2. What is the other speaker's professional role?
   - your colleague
   - your superior
   - your subordinate

3. What is the other speaker's age?
   - much older than you
   - much younger than you
   - about the same age

4. What is the setting?
   - a scientific conference
   - a business meeting
   - a staff picnic

5. What subject are you discussing?
   - typical work-related matters
   - a special favor that you want
   - a serious complaint

Of course, most speaking situations involve some or all of these factors, not just one. And your choice of language style will depend on how these factors combine. For example, how do the following differences change the appropriate language style?

1. You are in a committee meeting $\begin{cases} \text{with only your colleagues.} \\ \text{with a group of your superiors.} \end{cases}$

2. You are asking $\begin{cases} \text{your research assistant} \\ \text{your supervisor} \end{cases}$ for help with a project.

3. You are talking with a friend $\begin{cases} \text{about a lecture you attended.} \\ \text{about lending you a large amount of} \\ \quad \text{money.} \end{cases}$

Fortunately, much of the language that you learn is neutral in style. Therefore, you can use it in both formal and informal situations. However, as you improve your speaking ability, you will find it easier to change your speaking style according to the subject, the situation, and the people involved.

Discussion Techniques

INTRODUCING A DISCUSSION

An introduction to a discussion generally consists of several main points that the group leader can cover in a minute or two. The following is a list of points that are usually included in an introduction, along with some possible ways of expressing these points. Of course, you can also use your own words to convey these points:

- *Gaining attention*

    "Is everyone ready to begin?"
    "Why don't we get started?"

- *Greeting*

    "Good morning [afternoon, evening]."

- *General statement of the subject*

    "We're here today to talk about _____."

- *Statement of the specific purpose or goal of the discussion*

    "The $\left\{ \begin{array}{l} \text{purpose} \\ \text{goal} \end{array} \right\}$ of this discussion is to $\left\{ \begin{array}{l} \text{agree} \\ \text{decide} \\ \text{solve} \end{array} \right\}$ _____."

- *Introduction of the group members (if they do not know each other)*

    "At our meeting today we have Mike Smith, who is a government official. Also, we have _____."
    "Why don't you introduce yourselves?"

- *Opening up the subject for discussion*

    "Mary [or Dr. Jones], would you like to begin?"
    "Who would like to begin?"

Discussion Practice

SOLVING A PROBLEM

The cases in this section are designed to give you practice in participating in problem-solving discussions. The instructions included in this section apply to the cases in this unit as well as to those in Units 3, 6, 9, 11, 12, and 15. The cases in this unit (and Unit 3), however, provide more detailed information to guide you through the discussion process. By working step-by-step through one of the cases in this unit, you will learn how to prepare efficiently for all the problem-solving discussions in this book.

Instructions

1. *Choosing cases.* All groups may be assigned to work on the same case in order to compare solutions, or groups may work on different cases according to their particular backgrounds or interests. You should feel free to add details or change the cases to make them more closely suit your personal, professional, local, or national circumstances.

2. *Working with observers.* Your discussion may be observed by a student, several students, or the rest of the class, as directed by your instructor. Observers can complete the Observer Evaluation Form at the end of the unit or follow other instructions given by the teacher.

3. *Getting organized.* Get into small groups. Study the information presented in the case so that you have a clear understanding of the situation, purpose of the discussion, and group roles.

4. *Brainstorming.* In order to prepare for the discussion, you may work with members of your group, or you may form temporary "buzz" groups with two or three students from other groups working on the same case. One technique you can use to develop different ideas for a discussion is called brainstorming. In a brainstorming session, you "think aloud" in a small group by stating ideas as they come to mind. Here are points to keep in mind during brainstorming:

   - In five or ten minutes make a list of as many ideas as possible.
   - Get everyone in the group actively involved.
   - Remember that quantity is more important than quality.
   - Feel free to suggest any idea, even if it seems stupid or crazy.
   - Try to build on or add to ideas suggested by others.
   - To encourage creative thinking, do not judge any idea mentioned.
   - Write down all ideas without comment.

   Each case in Units 2 and 3 includes specific points to guide you during brainstorming.

5. *Selecting ideas.* Consider all the ideas from the brainstorming session. Participants in the group discussion are likely to support some of these ideas more than others because of their particular interests or points of view. The group leader, however, would probably not show strong support of any ideas in advance, be-

cause his or her job is to help the group consider all ideas fairly and objectively. After your group has brainstormed a long list of possible ideas, work together to select the best ones for each role. Each case in Unit 2 includes a chart to help you organize ideas for the discussion. At this point, students working in buzz groups can return to their original groups.

6. *Preparing for the discussion.* Now you choose or are assigned a specific role in the discussion: one student as group leader, one or two students in each of the other roles, and one or more observers (if desired). Participants should take a few minutes to think of facts, reasons, and examples to support the ideas developed earlier for their particular role. The group leader can use this time to plan an appropriate introduction, review the guidelines for closing a discussion (Unit 3), and/or study the responsibilities of an effective leader (Unit 5). Group observers should look over the Observer Evaluation Form included at the end of the unit.

7. *Starting the discussion.* Your group is now ready to begin the discussion. If observers are involved, the instructor may set shorter time limits so that they do not lose interest. Whatever the time limits, do not hurry through the discussion simply to find a quick solution to the problem. The goal of the discussion is for you to improve your interaction skills. Thus, what you learn from working with others in English is more important than the actual solution you reach.

8. *Follow-up to the discussion.* After participating in the discussion, all group members can complete the Participation Self-Evaluation Form on page 34. Group observers should complete the Observer Evaluation Form on page 36 as directed by the instructor. They can then discuss their evaluations with the group members. If other groups have worked on the same case, compare your solutions.

CASE 1: A MILLION DOLLAR DONATION

Situation

An anonymous donor has given one million dollars to the National Institute of Technology. The purpose of this donation is "to improve the overall quality of scientific education provided by the institute."

The donor has indicated that the money should be spent on one major project that will have a strong effect on the quality of education. If the money is well-spent, the donor is very likely to give even more money in the future. A committee has been formed to make a formal recommendation as to how the money should be spent. A meeting has been called to discuss the issue.

Purpose of the Discussion

Group members should try to agree on the best way to spend the one million dollars.

Group Roles

The following people take part in the discussion:

> Leader: the president of the institute
> Representative(s) of the faculty
> Representative(s) of the students
> Representative(s) of the administration

Brainstorming

What are different ways that the institute can spend the money? Work with other members of your group or in a buzz group to brainstorm as many ideas as possible. You can use the following list to help you think of possible people or organizations ("agents") that might be able to take some action regarding the situation. In addition, the information under "actions" includes useful verbs and other vocabulary to guide you in developing a number of possible ideas. Since the information provided is not complete, you will have to add more details to develop these ideas into specific points. Of course, you can also add your own ideas.

Agents	Actions	
the institute	increase	number of departments
		size of faculty
		salaries
	sponsor	trips to conferences
	subsidize	
	give	research grants
	provide	scholarships
		free books
	build	laboratories
	improve	classrooms
	modernize	computer center
	enlarge	library
	expand	

Specific Solutions

1. *The institute should build a modern computer center.*

2. _____

3. _____

4. _____

5. _____

6. _____

7. _____

8. _____

9. _____

10. _____

Selecting Ideas

Consider the ideas that you developed during the brainstorming session. You can use the following chart to list the best ideas for each role:

Representative(s) *of faculty*	*Representative(s)* *of students*	*Representative(s)* *of administration*

Starting the Discussion

After you have chosen or been assigned a role in the discussion, spend a few minutes preparing your ideas. Your group can then begin the discussion, keeping in mind any time limits set by the instructor.

CASE 2: DYING FORESTS

Situation

In a certain country, 20 percent of the trees are dying. Automobile emissions have been identified as the primary factor. A leading scientist has estimated that unless auto emissions are reduced, 60 percent of the trees in the country's forests will be killed or damaged within four years. Forestry engineers want the government to enact a 60 mile/100 kilometer per hour speed limit throughout the country. They say that such a speed limit will cut emissions significantly and save the trees. Many motorists are against the forestry engineers' recommendation. These drivers do not want the government to put any restrictions on their freedom. They believe that there must be other ways to solve the problem and are in favor of more research. The government has called a meeting to discuss the issue.

Purpose of the Discussion

Group members should try to agree on the best way to stop or reduce the destruction of the forest.

Group Roles

The following people take part in the discussion:

> Leader: a representative of the government
> Forestry engineer(s)
> Motorist(s)

Brainstorming

What are different ways to stop or reduce the destruction of the forest? Work with members of your group or in a buzz group to brainstorm as many ideas as possible. You can use the following list to help you think of possible people or organizations ("agents") that might be able to take some action regarding the situation. In addition, the information under "actions" includes useful verbs and other vocabulary to guide you in developing a number of possible ideas. Since the information provided is not complete, you will have to add more details to develop these ideas into specific points. Of course, you can also add your own ideas.

Agents	*Actions*	
the government	plant	trees resistant to pollution
forestry engineers		
drivers	require	unleaded gasoline
citizens		catalytic converters
	restrict	number of cars
	limit	use of cars
		access to roads
	lower	speed limits
	decrease	
	reduce	
	reforest	area
	impose	gasoline rationing system
	improve	public transportation

Specific Solutions

1. *The government can plant trees resistant to pollution*.
2. _____
3. _____
4. _____
5. _____
6. _____
7. _____
8. _____
9. _____
10. _____

Selecting Ideas

Consider the different ideas that you developed during the brainstorming session. Select the best ideas from the list for each role:

Forestry engineers | *Motorists*

Starting the Discussion

After you have chosen or been assigned a role in the discussion, spend a few minutes preparing your ideas. Your group can then begin the discussion, keeping in mind any time limits set by the instructor.

CASE 3: PREVENTING WASTE

Situation

A country is struggling to dispose of growing mountains of refuse, much of it poisonous, that have been dumped in landfills across the nation. Along with most other countries of the world, this nation faces an urgent dilemma: how to reduce the huge amounts of waste by-products without endangering human health or damaging the environment. When garbage is burned, it discharges dangerous gases into the air. Landfill sites, where garbage and industrial wastes are dumped, often contain hazardous wastes that leach into groundwater supplies, contaminating drinking water and polluting farmland. Since there are few methods of effective waste disposal, government officials feel that it is essential to involve consumers and manufacturers in reducing the amount of waste that is produced. A meeting has been called to discuss the issue.

Purpose of the Discussion

⋆ Group members should try to agree on the best way to reduce the amount of waste produced in this country.

Group Roles

The following people take part in the discussion:

> Leader: a government official
> Consumer representative(s)
> Representative(s) of manufacturers

Brainstorming

What are different ways to reduce the amount of waste that is produced? Work with members of your group or in a buzz group to brainstorm as many ideas as possible. You can use the following list to help you think of possible people or organizations ("agents") that might be able to take some action regarding the situation. In addition, the information under "actions" includes useful verbs and other vocabulary to guide you in developing a number of possible ideas. Since the information provided is not complete, you will have to add more details to develop these ideas into specific points. Of course, you can also add your own ideas.

Agents	Actions	
the government federal agencies manufacturers companies consumers households	increase	use of recycled paper products number of collection points variety of containers that can be returned for cash
	sort	garbage into recyclable and nonrecyclable items
	raise	price of garbage collection price of toxic-waste removal reward for return of recyclable items
	impose	harsh penalties for improper disposal high fines for excessive production of wastes
	use	fewer toxic chemicals
	sponsor	media campaign to encourage recycling

Specific Solutions

1. *City governments should raise the price of garbage collection.*

2. _____

3. _____

4. _____

5. _____

6. _____

7. _____

8. _____

9. _____

10. _____

Selecting Ideas

Consider the different ideas that you developed during the brain-storming session. Select the best ideas from the list for each role:

Consumer representatives	*Representatives of manufacturers*

Starting the Discussion

After you have chosen or been assigned a role in the discussion, spend a few minutes preparing your ideas. Your group can then begin the discussion, keeping in mind any time limits set by the instructor.

CASE 4: GOOD HEALTH

Situation

The National Health Association has recently published a report showing that the people in the nation are physically unfit. This study indicates that at least one third of the population is in a high-risk category. This means that they are very likely to have health problems in the future. Furthermore, according to the report, many complaints and ailments, such as chronic fatigue or even the common cold, could be avoided if people took better care of their health.

Business leaders in the community have asked the government to do something about this problem. They are particularly concerned because of the large number of lost workdays, which costs them a lot of money. A meeting has been called by the local government to discuss the issue.

Purpose of the Discussion

Group members should try to agree on the best way to encourage citizens to take care of their health.

Group Roles

The following people take part in the discussion:

> Leader: a representative of the local government
> Company representative(s)
> Health professional(s)

Brainstorming

What are different ways that the community can improve the health of its citizens? Work with members of your group or in a buzz group to brainstorm as many ideas as possible. You can use the following list to help you think of possible people or organizations ("agents") that might be able to take some action regarding the situation. In addition, the information under "actions" includes useful verbs and other vocabulary to guide you in developing a number of possible ideas. Since the information provided is not complete, you will have to add more details to develop these ideas into specific points. Of course, you can also add your own ideas.

Agents	Actions	
companies	build	fitness centers
businesses	improve	sports clubs
educators	enlarge	
the government	expand	
physicians		
health	sponsor	family fun runs
professionals	promote	marathons
community	support	fitness testing
organizations	subsidize	health week activities
		an advertising campaign
		regular physical exams
		exercise programs
	give	public lectures
	provide	school programs

Specific Solutions

1. *Companies should build fitness centers for their employees.*
2. _____
3. _____
4. _____
5. _____
6. _____
7. _____
8. _____
9. _____
10. _____

Selecting Ideas

Consider the different ideas that you developed during the brain-storming session. Select the best ideas from the list for each role:

Company representatives | *Health professionals*

Starting the Discussion

After you have chosen or been assigned a role in the discussion, spend a few minutes preparing your ideas. Your group can then begin the discussion, keeping in mind any time limits set by the instructor.

Discussion Evaluation

A. PARTICIPANT SELF-EVALUATION FORM

After you participate in a group discussion, answer the following questions by putting a check [✓] in the appropriate spaces.

1. When you spoke, how often did you use English?

    _____ A. All of the time.

    _____ B. Most of the time.

    _X_ C. Some of the time.

    _____ D. None of the time.

2. How many times did you have a chance to speak during the discussion?

    _____ A. Five or more times.

    _____ B. Three or four times.

    _X_ C. One or two times.

    _____ D. None.

3. How many questions did you ask?

    _____ A. Five or more.

    _____ B. Three or four.

    _X_ C. One or two.

    _____ D. None.

4. How many different expressions from the unit did you use?

    _____ A. Five or more.

    _____ B. Three or four.

    _X_ C. One or two.

    _____ D. None.

5. Did you have any problems during the discussion? Check any of the following that apply to you:

    _____ A. I didn't understand the topic.

    _X_ B. I didn't know enough about the topic to contribute ideas.

_X_ C. I couldn't think of anything to say.

_X_ D. I had problems with vocabulary. I didn't know the right words in English to say what I wanted.

_X_ E. I had problems with grammar.

_X_ F. I had some problems with my pronunciation.

_____ G. I haven't had enough practice in speaking English and I just couldn't get the words out.

_X_ H. It was difficult to use the expressions from the unit.

_____ I. Other speakers interrupted me.

_____ J. Other speakers didn't give me a chance to talk.

_X_ K. I felt nervous or shy.

_____ L. Nobody paid attention to what I said.

_____ M. I couldn't understand the other speakers.

_____ N. I think I talked too much.

_____ O. _____

6. How can you solve the problems that you checked?

X Can solve the problems by trying to ask question and practice to speak English all time, so it helps me to pronounce right. X should involve more with group discussion

7. Overall, how do you think your group did? Use the following scale to rate the discussion:

Overall Performance. In general, how was the discussion?

Excellent	Satisfactory	Weak	Unsatisfactory
3	2	1	0

(1 circled)

8. How do you think you can improve the next discussion?

X have more chance to practice and express my opion

more clearly

B. OBSERVER EVALUATION FORM

1. *Identifying the group*

   A. Discussion topic: _____

   B. Names of students in group: _____

   _____

2. *Listening to the discussion.* As you listen, make a list of the possible solutions that the group members discuss.

   _____

   _____

   _____

   _____

   _____

3. *Rating the group.* At the end of the discussion, use the following scales to rate the discussion group:

   A. *Participation.* Did all group members interact and take equal part in the discussion?

Excellent	Satisfactory	Weak	Unsatisfactory
3	2	1	0

   B. *Clarity.* Did all group members speak loudly and clearly?

Excellent	Satisfactory	Weak	Unsatisfactory
3	2	1	0

4. *Making suggestions.* What suggestions can you make to help the group improve the next discussion?

   _____

   _____

   _____

   _____

Handling Suggestions

Expressions

The following list includes only some of the many possible expressions used to convey each function. Space is provided for you to add other expressions related to each function as you work through the unit. Before going over the lists provided, you may want to discuss each function and then work individually or in small groups to list expressions that you are already familiar with. You can identify any expressions that seem to be particularly formal, informal, direct, or indirect and then compare them with those listed here. You might also discuss possible situations in which these expressions could appropriately be used.

Making a suggestion
Let's _____.
Perhaps we could _____.
We might _____.
Why don't we _____?
Why not _____?
What about _____?
How about _____?
I suggest that we _____.

Accepting a suggestion
  Yes, of course.
  Certainly.
  By all means.
  Yes, that's a good idea.
  Yes, why don't we try that?

Rejecting a suggestion
  Unfortunately, _____.
  I'm sorry, but _____.
  Well, the problem is _____.

  I'm not sure that idea will $\begin{Bmatrix} \text{be possible} \\ \text{work} \end{Bmatrix}$ because _____.

  Note: When you reject or show doubt about a suggestion, you
  should try to explain your reason(s) to the person making the
  suggestion.

Showing doubt
  Well, . . . ummm . . . maybe . . .
  Well, . . . possibly . . .
  Yes, . . . perhaps . . .
  I don't know.
  Well, I'm just not sure.

Listening Practice

The following exercises can be completed by listening to Unit 3 on the
tape.

Section 1.   There is one discussion in this section. City officials are
brainstorming possible solutions to a problem.

A.   Listen to Section 1 on the tape. In this discussion, what problem
are the group members trying to solve?

_____

B.   Listen again. What suggestions do the speakers have? Make a
list of these suggestions in the order that you hear them.

Suggestions   *Expressions*

1. _____   _____

2. _____   _____

3. _____   _____

4. _____   _____

5. _____   _____

C.   Listen a third time. What expressions do the speakers use to introduce the suggestions? Write the expression next to each suggestion.

D.   Work with a partner, in a small group, or as a class to compare your answers.

Section 2.   In this section you will hear six separate dialogs about the same subject. Agricultural specialists and government officials are discussing the problem of low agricultural output.

A.   Listen to Section 2 on the tape. What suggestions are offered in each dialog to solve the problem? Write the suggestion that each speaker offers.

Suggestions

1. _____

2. _____

3. _____

4. _____

5. _____

6. _____

B.   Work with a partner, in a small group, or as a class to compare your answers.

C.   Listen again. Is the suggestion accepted or rejected in each dialog? Put a check [✔] in the correct space.

Accept   *Reject*   *Expressions*

1. _____   _____   _____

2. _____   _____   _____

	Accept	*Reject*	*Expressions*
3.	_____	_____	_____
4.	_____	_____	_____
5.	_____	_____	_____
6.	_____	_____	_____

D. Listen a third time. Write the expression that the speaker uses to accept or reject each suggestion.

E. Work with a partner, in a small group, or as a class to compare your answers.

Controlled Practice

Exercise 1. Use different expressions from the unit in discussing the illustrations on page 42.

> *Speaker A:* Make a suggestion based on each picture.
>
> *Speaker B:* Accept, reject, or show doubt about the suggestion.

Exercise 2. Use a variety of expressions from the unit in discussing the following situations.

> *Student A:* Make a suggestion to deal with the situation.
>
> *Student B:* Accept, reject, or show doubt about the suggestion. If you reject the suggestion, give a reason.

General Interest

1. *(colleague to colleague)* The Science Institute is offering a weekend workshop in your field. You are both interested in attending it.
2. *(consultant to consultant)* Work is behind schedule. The project will not be completed on the required date.
3. *(friend to friend)* Your friend is having trouble sleeping at night.
4. *(supervisor to supervisor)* Production levels are low.
5. *(researcher to research assistant)* Several animals used in experiments have died.
6. *(colleague to colleague)* Your colleague's car won't start.
7. *(employee to supervisor)* The response time on your terminal is too slow.

8. *(administrator to administrator)* Technicians have asked for in-service training.
9. *(friend to friend)* Your friend is trying to stop smoking.
10. *(employee to director)* A piece of equipment is not working properly.

Science

11. *(manager to secretary)* The leaves on the plants in the office are turning yellow.
12. *(consultant to director)* Mildew has begun to attack many books in the library.
13. *(consultant to consultant)* Oil from a nearby oil spill is being washed onto the beaches.
14. *(colleague to colleague)* The company you work for has violated a safety requirement.
15. *(friend to friend)* You are swimming and see lightning in the distance.

Engineering

16. *(employee to executive)* The water supply is contaminated due to the improper disposal of sewage.
17. *(supervisor to supervisor)* Several construction crew accidents have occurred recently.
18. *(colleague to colleague)* A proposed highway will have to go through a residential area.
19. *(colleague to colleague)* A metal is needed that will conduct electricity.
20. *(colleague to colleague)* A cold, icy winter has badly damaged the city's roads.

Health

21. *(colleague to colleague)* A patient is not responding to antibiotic treatment.
22. *(supervisor to employee)* There is a flu epidemic.
23. *(consultant to consultant)* A couple wants a child. They are afraid of passing on an inherited disease.
24. *(colleague to colleague)* A patient is asking for a drug to relieve his pain.
25. *(supervisor to supervisor)* The number of cases of food poisoning has increased in the past two months.

Any Suggestions?

1. a disorganized laboratory

2. a littered picnic area

3. a heavy load

4. car trouble

Exercise 3. Use a variety of expressions from the unit in discussing the following situations.

> *Student A:* Make a suggestion based on the situation.
>
> *Student B:* Accept, reject, or show doubt about the suggestion.
>
> *Student C:* Make another suggestion.
>
> *Student D:* Accept, reject, or show doubt about the suggestion.

General Interest

1. how to limit residents' use of electricity during peak periods
2. how to improve English class
3. how to encourage the use of public transportation
4. how to motivate workers
5. how to keep up to date in a particular field of specialization

Science

6. how to improve crop yields
7. how to prevent the loss of wildlife
8. how to reduce water consumption
9. how to prevent computer crime
10. how to increase student enrollment in astrophysics

Engineering

11. how to build a fuel-efficient house
12. how to increase the speed of ships in the water
13. how to reduce the noise of jet engines
14. how to lengthen the life of a battery
15. how to make cheaper cars

Health

16. how to get children to take medicine
17. how to reduce the risk of getting a cold
18. how to encourage men to become nurses
19. how to reduce cholesterol levels in your blood
20. how to improve the handling of patients' records

Communication Concepts

EFFECTIVE MEETINGS

The following are guidelines for more effective meetings:

1. All participants should be informed in advance of the time, place, and probable length of the meeting. This should be done in writing, if possible.
2. A written agenda is useful if there are several points to be discussed. This agenda should include the topics to be discussed and their order. Meetings usually run more smoothly when participants know in advance which topics will be covered.
3. Even if an agenda is not provided, the group should have a specific purpose or goal to guide the discussion. After the group leader gives a clear statement of the goal of the meeting, all group members share responsibility for accomplishing this goal.
4. Time limits for the meeting should be set in advance. The meeting should start and end at the scheduled time.
5. Discussion group members should be present and ready to start on time.
6. Once the meeting starts, participants should not leave the room except for an emergency. Other participants may feel annoyed if people leave for routine matters such as making telephone calls or talking to visitors.
7. The meeting should be an honest, open exchange of ideas. This means that group members should expect and encourage differences of opinion. In fact, disagreements are useful since they help members look at different sides of an issue before making a decision. Members cannot learn from one another by agreeing all the time.
8. When discussion group members are from different cultures, they should be especially careful that they understand each other. Silence, for example, may show agreement or it may show total disagreement. The word "yes" can mean that the person agrees, or it can mean simply that the person understands what is being said. Therefore, it may be necessary for participants to ask more questions to make sure that they understand what the others are thinking.
9. Discussion group members should consider the different ways of reaching a decision.
   A. *Consensus.* The group members reach a general agreement through discussion.

      B. *Majority rule.* Although all of the participants may not agree, the group chooses a solution that more than half of the people agree on.

      C. *Voting.* Since there is no clear majority of people in favor of a particular solution, the group members vote and the solution with the most votes wins.

      D. *Authority.* The leader or a strong participant makes or pushes through a decision.

      E. *Default.* The group is unable to make a decision.

   10. If possible, participants should try to reach a consensus. Clearly, the best decision is one that all group members can agree on.

Discussion Techniques

CLOSING A DISCUSSION

In ending the discussion, most group leaders briefly cover several main points. The exact closing, however, depends on what happened during the discussion. The following are the points that are usually included in the closing along with some possible ways of expressing these points. Of course, you can also use your own words to convey these points.

- *A statement that the meeting time is over*

  "I'm afraid that we'll have to end here. Unfortunately, we've run out of time."

  "Excuse me, it looks like our time is up."

- *A final summary of the discussion*

  What conclusions were reached:

  "To summarize, we $\left\{ \begin{array}{l} \text{agreed} \\ \text{decided} \end{array} \right\}$ that ＿＿＿＿＿＿."

  What was accomplished if no conclusions were reached:

  "Well, we weren't able to make a final decision, but I think that we accomplished a lot today. We ＿＿＿＿＿＿."

- *A plan for a future meeting if the problem is not solved*

  "We can discuss this further at our next meeting."

  "Could we have a meeting soon to continue discussion of this subject?"

- *A statement to thank the members for their participation in the discussion*

  "Thank you all for coming."
  "I'd like to thank you all for your cooperation."

Discussion Practice

SOLVING A PROBLEM

The cases in this section will give you further practice in participating in problem-solving discussions.

Instructions

1. Refer to the detailed instructions included in the Discussion Practice section of Unit 2 for guidance in choosing cases, getting organized, brainstorming, selecting ideas, preparing for, and starting the discussion. In order to keep the discussion moving in an organized way, your group should try to analyze one proposed solution in detail before moving on to discuss the next one. Examine each solution carefully to discover both its advantages and disadvantages.
2. Group observers should complete the Observer Evaluation Form on page 55 as directed by the instructor. They can then discuss their evaluations with the group members. If other groups have worked on the same case, compare your solutions.

CASE 1: ENDANGERED MARINE LIFE

Situation

Large numbers of whales, penguins, and seals face destruction because of oil pollution. Spills from drilling accidents at offshore installations have created oil slicks that are deadly for these marine animals. The Center for Marine Emergency Action wants the government to stop oil exploration in the areas inhabited by the endangered animals. The head of the center says that it is a crime to drill for oil in an area with such spectacular wildlife. Oil companies feel that the scientists at the center are not being practical. Oil is necessary for the country's economy. They believe that the scientists should concentrate on trying to use technology to fight oil pollution. A meeting has been called to discuss the situation.

Purpose of the Discussion

Group members should try to agree on the best way to use this area.

Group Roles

The following people take part in the discussion:

> Leader: a representative of the government
> Representative(s) of the Center for Marine Emergency Action
> Representative(s) of the oil companies

Brainstorming

What are different ways to solve the problem? Work with members of your group or in a buzz group to brainstorm as many ideas as possible. You can use the following list to help you think of possible people or organizations ("agents") that might be able to take some action regarding the situation. In addition, the information under "actions" includes useful verbs and other vocabulary to guide you in developing a number of possible ideas. Since the information provided is not complete, you will have to add more details to develop these ideas into specific points. Of course, you can also add your own ideas. Write the ideas from this brainstorming session on a separate sheet of paper.

Agents	*Actions*	
the government	control	oil companies
the Center for Marine Emergency Action	impose	penalties
oil companies	choose	alternative sites
environmentalists	select	
	ban	oil exploration
	forbid	
	prohibit	
	restrict	
	limit	
	relocate	animals
	move	
	invest in	technology for prevention
		technology for cleanup

Selecting Ideas

Consider the different ideas that you developed during the brain-storming session. Select the best ideas from the list for each role and write them on a separate sheet of paper.

Starting the Discussion

After you have chosen or been assigned a role in the discussion, spend a few minutes preparing your ideas. Your group can then begin the discussion, keeping in mind any time limits set by the instructor.

CASE 2: COMPUTERIZATION

Situation

The administration of a polytechnic institute has decided to implement a new policy. At the beginning of the next academic year, first-year students will be required to purchase personal computers. All assignments must be done on computers. Administrators, faculty members, and students agree that the ability to use computers is necessary to be competitive in the fields of science and technology. The students, however, say that they cannot afford the added expense of personal computers. Administrators and faculty members, on the other hand, see buying computers as the students' investment in their future. Faculty members from the institute are meeting with administration officials to discuss this new policy. Students have asked to be represented at this meeting.

Purpose of the Discussion

Group members should try to agree on the best way to train students so that they can make use of computer technology.

Group Roles

The following people take part in the discussion:

> Leader: a representative from the administration
> Representative(s) of the institute faculty
> Representative(s) of the students

Brainstorming

What are different ways to solve the problem? Work with members of your group or in a buzz group to brainstorm as many ideas as possible. You can use the following list to help you think of possible people or organizations ("agents") that might be able to take some action regarding the situation. In addition, the information under "actions" includes useful verbs and other vocabulary to guide you in developing a number of possible ideas. Since the information provided is not complete, you will have to add more details to develop these ideas into specific points. Of course, you can also add your own ideas. Write the ideas from this brainstorming session on a separate sheet of paper.

Agents	Actions	
the administration	provide	computer facilities in convenient locations
faculty members		
students		discount prices
local stores	require	computer courses
computer companies		
	offer	optional computer courses
		peer tutoring
	involve	scientific community
	sponsor	computer clubs
	promote	
	subsidize	
	support	

Selecting Ideas

Consider the different ideas that you developed during the brain-storming session. Select the best ideas from the list for each role and write them on a separate sheet of paper.

Starting the Discussion

After you have chosen or been assigned a role in the discussion, spend a few minutes preparing your ideas. Your group can then begin the discussion, keeping in mind any time limits set by the instructor.

CASE 3: THREATENED HISTORICAL SITE

Situation

Two-thousand-year-old treasures will soon be destroyed if a city builds a planned highway through an ancient site. The Traffic Department of this city says that this highway is necessary to relieve congested city streets. However, the proposed highway will run within a few feet of the world-famous historical site. In fact, according to the Traffic Department's plans, the highway will run through the middle of an unexcavated temple. Archaeologists oppose the plan. They say that the treasures of the temple will be lost forever if the highway is built. They also argue that vibration and pollution caused by traffic will weaken all of the ancient ruins. Business people in town fear that the loss of the ruins will result in a loss of tourism and thus a loss in income for the town. Traffic department engineers claim that the project will not cause any damage to the ancient site and that alternative routes will disrupt residential areas. A meeting has been called to discuss the situation.

Purpose of the Discussion

Group members should try to agree on the best action to take regarding the highway.

Group Roles

The following people take part in the discussion:

> Leader: a representative of the government
> Engineer(s) from the Traffic Department
> Archaeologist(s)
> Business representative(s)

Brainstorming

What are different ways to solve the problem? Work with members of your group or in a buzz group to brainstorm as many ideas as possible. You can use the following list to help you think of possible people or organizations ("agents") that might be able to take some action regarding the situation. In addition, the information under "actions" includes useful verbs and other vocabulary to guide you in developing a number of possible ideas. Since the information provided is not complete, you will have to add more details to develop these ideas into specific points. Of course, you can also add your own ideas. Write the ideas from this brainstorming session on a separate sheet of paper.

Agents	Actions	
Traffic Department engineers	improve expand promote	public transportation
archaeologists businesses residents the local government the national government	move relocate enclose	ruins
	restrict limit	use of cars
	abandon ban prohibit	building of highway
	build	bridge over ruins
	plan	alternative route(s)
	decrease	size of highway

Selecting Ideas

Consider the different ideas that you developed during the brainstorming session. Select the best ideas from the list for each role and write them on a separate sheet of paper.

Starting the Discussion

After you have chosen or been assigned a role in the discussion, spend a few minutes preparing your ideas. Your group can then begin the discussion, keeping in mind any time limits set by the instructor.

CASE 4: ANTI-SMOKING MEASURES

Situation

Smoking is responsible for more than one million deaths a year. Its victims include nonsmokers as well as smokers. In fact, tobacco smoke in the air can lead to lung cancer, heart disease, and respiratory problems. Nonsmokers exposed to cigarette smoke are very much at risk, according to recent evidence released by the Department of Health. To reduce the number of smoke-related illnesses the Department of Health has called for a smoke-free society. The department wants the government to ban smoking in all public places including stores, offices, and restaurants. Smokers feel that a total ban is too strict. They say smokers have rights too. A meeting has been called to discuss the situation.

Purpose of the Discussion

Group members should try to agree on the most effective measures to reduce environmental tobacco smoke.

Group Roles

The following people take part in the discussion:

> Leader: a representative of the government
> Representative(s) of the Department of Health
> Smoker(s)
> Nonsmoker(s)

Brainstorming

What are different ways to reduce tobacco smoke in the environment? Work with members of your group or in a buzz group to brainstorm as many ideas as possible. You can use the following list to help you think of possible people or organizations ("agents") that might be able to take some action regarding the situation. In addition, the information under "actions" includes useful verbs and other vocabulary to guide you in developing a number of possible ideas. Since the information provided is not complete, you will have to add more details to develop these ideas into specific points. Of course, you can also add your own ideas. Write the ideas from this brainstorming session on a separate sheet of paper.

Agents	Actions	
the government	limit	smoking areas
smokers	restrict	
nonsmokers		
businesses	provide	separate smoking
companies		areas
schools	sponsor	public lectures
the local media	promote	media campaigns
	support	school programs
	subsidize	
	reward	nonsmokers
	penalize	smokers
	ban	smoking in all
	prohibit	public places
	forbid	
	encourage	voluntary ban

Selecting Ideas

Consider the different ideas that you developed during the brainstorming session. Select the best ideas from the list for each role and write them on a separate sheet of paper.

Starting the Discussion

After you have chosen or been assigned a role in the discussion, spend a few minutes preparing your ideas. Your group can then begin the discussion, keeping in mind any time limits set by the instructor.

Discussion Evaluation

OBSERVER EVALUATION FORM

1. *Identifying the group*

A. Discussion topic: _____

B. Names of students in group: _____

_____

2. *Listening to the discussion.* As you listen, make a list of the possible solutions that the group members discuss.

_____

_____

_____

_____

_____

3. *Rating the group.* At the end of the discussion, use the following scales to rate the discussion group:

A. *Participation.* Did all group members interact and take equal part in the discussion?

Excellent	Satisfactory	Weak	Unsatisfactory
3	2	1	0

B. *Pace.* Did the discussion move along at the right speed, without long pauses between speakers?

Excellent	Satisfactory	Weak	Unsatisfactory
3	2	1	0

4. *Making suggestions.* What suggestions can you make to help group members improve their next discussion?

_____

_____

_____

_____

Determining Content

Presentation Preparation

DETERMINING THE CONTENT

When you think about how to give your presentation, you are concerned with delivery. When you think about what information to include in your presentation, you are concerned with content.

A. Selecting and Limiting Your Topic

In a professional situation the topic of your presentation is usually determined by the needs of your listeners. You may be asked to provide certain information because of your specialized knowledge or your experience in a particular area. For example, you might have to demonstrate how something works, describe a technical process, compare two pieces of equipment made by different companies, or give on-the-job instructions.

A classroom situation differs from a professional situation in that you often have more freedom to choose your own topic for a class presentation. Of course, you should choose a topic that you already know something about, one that interests you, and one that is of potential interest to your listeners. You can choose a subject related to your work, your studies, your research projects, or your personal interests. Current events or social issues can also make good subjects for class presentations. Once you have chosen a general subject area, then you have to limit your topic so you can cover it adequately within the time available for your presentation. It is usually more effective to give a detailed explanation of a specific, limited topic than to try to cover too much material in a short time. When selecting your own topic for a class presentation, you should consider the following points:

1. Do you know enough about this topic?
2. If some research is needed, do you have the time and resources to find the information?
3. Have you limited the topic enough so that you can cover it adequately in the time available?
4. Is this topic of potential interest to your listeners?
5. Is the topic too difficult or too technical for this audience?
6. Is the topic too easy or too well-known to this audience?

B. Determining Your General Purpose

In giving a presentation, a speaker usually has one of three general purposes: to inform, to persuade, or to entertain the listeners. Most of the oral presentations that you need to give at work are reports to inform your listeners—to give them information that they want or need to know. Therefore, the focus in this course is on informative presentations. Your goal in giving any type of informative presentation is to communicate useful information in a clear way.

C. Analyzing the Audience

Whenever you give a presentation, you should always find out as much as possible about your listeners' background and knowledge. This gives you the advantage of being able to adapt your presentation to suit the special needs and interests of the particular people you are speaking to. The type of people in your audience will affect the vocabulary you use, the kinds of examples you select, and the amount of background and technical information you include. In analyzing a particular group of listeners, you should try to answer the following questions:

Who Are Your Listeners?
By finding common areas of interest that your listeners share, you can choose details or examples that relate to these interests. You might consider the following characteristics:

- *Occupation.* Are most of your listeners in the same or related occupations? Do they work for the same company?
- *Position in organization.* Do most of your listeners have administrative or technical backgrounds? Are they managers, management trainees, new employees, technicians, or clerical staff?
- *Level of education.* What is the highest level of education of most of your listeners: high school diploma? bachelor's degree? master's degree? Ph.D.?
- *Area of specialization.* If your listeners all work in one general field, what are their areas of specialization?
- *Special interests.* Do your listeners belong to the same professional organization, special interest group, or social club?
- *Age, sex, income level, nationality.* Are the listeners mainly young or old, male or female, of the same income level, or of one nationality? Are any of these factors significant in finding common areas of interest among your listeners?

What Is the General Level of English of the Listeners?
In order to make your message clear, you need to use language that the audience can understand. If most of your listeners are not native speakers of English, then you must be especially careful to use vocabulary words that most of them will know. It will not be effective to use new or difficult vocabulary words if your listeners cannot understand them. If you think that many people may not know the meaning of a few technical or specialized words you consider essential, then you might write these words on the board before you begin your presentation. Of course, you can always explain a few unfamiliar words as you go along; however, keep in mind that interrupting your presentation to define or explain many new words may make it difficult for your listeners to follow the flow of your ideas.

How Much Technical Background Do the Listeners Have?
By knowing how much technical information your listeners can understand, you can appropriately adjust the technical content of your presentation.

- If most of your listeners are experts with specialized training similar to your own, they will understand and expect highly technical data.
- Listeners with a technical background may be familiar with your general subject area but may not be experts in your par-

ticular field. These people know many basic technical terms but will need explanations of specialized concepts.

- With listeners who have no technical background, you will have to use simple, nontechnical language with explanations of any technical concepts that you include in your presentation.
- When your listeners have mixed technical backgrounds, you should identify the lowest level of technical understanding and address yourself to this level.
- If you have no idea of the technical background of your audience, you should speak to them as a general audience.

How Much Do the Listeners Already Know about the Subject?
By knowing the background of your listeners, you can build your presentation on what they already know. Clearly, you do not want to waste your listeners' time by repeating information they already know. Also, you should know how much and what kind of background information to supply in order for them to understand your presentation.

What Do the Listeners Expect from Your Presentation?
When someone asks you to give a presentation, you need to know exactly what that person expects from you. For example, are you supposed to explain the principles of how a machine works or actually teach your listeners how to operate the machine? In order to be successful, your presentation has to meet the wants or needs of the audience. Before planning your presentation, make sure you know the answers to these questions:

- What do the listeners want or need to know?
- When is the presentation due?
- How long should the presentation be?
- Are there any special guidelines you should follow?

What Other Details of the Speaking Situation Might Affect Your Presentation?
You can make your presentation more effective by knowing as much as possible about the speaking situation in advance. Some of the following factors may influence the way you plan your presentation:

- How many people will you be speaking to?
- How will your listeners be seated—in rows, a circle, around a conference table, or another way?

- Will you be expected to stand in front of your listeners, sit at a desk in front of them, or sit with them around a large table?
- Will the situation be formal or informal?
- Where will your presentation be given? Will you be in your office, a classroom, or a lecture hall?
- What facilities (such as lectern, blackboard, slide projector, overhead projector, screen, video recorder) will be available?

ACTIVITY 4-A

1. Work in small groups. Using Worksheet 2 on page 246 of Appendix I, analyze your class as an audience. A sample worksheet following Worksheet 2 is included for your reference.
2. Discuss how your particular audience will affect your choice of topics for in-class presentations.
3. When all the groups have finished, compare the results of your worksheets.

ACTIVITY 4-B

1. Work individually to consider a group of people that you have spoken to in the past or that you might speak to in the future. Using a copy of Worksheet 2 on page 246, analyze this group as an audience.
2. Work in small groups. Take turns describing your audience to the group. Discuss how this particular audience affected (or will affect) your presentation. Did this audience cause you any special problems? Compare this audience and your class as an audience. How are they similar? How are they different?

ACTIVITY 4-C

1. Imagine that speakers have suggested a number of possible topics for oral presentations. The speakers who have proposed these topics are experts in their fields, so they have the necessary information to speak knowledgeably on their topics.

2. Work in small groups. Indicate whether the following topics would be satisfactory (S) or unsatisfactory (U) as ten- to fifteen-minute presentations to be given to your class. In analyzing each topic, consider whether it is (a) too limited, (b) too general, (c) too technical, or (d) too well known for the students in your class. If the topic is unsatisfactory, indicate what the problem is.

_C_ A. Alzheimer's disease
_a_ B. an explanation of the carbon cycle
_a_ C. reasons that industrial pollution is increasing in China
_C_ D. recent advances in using anti-idiotypic antibodies to fight viral diseases
_S_ E. pollution
_U_ F. possible effects of a fuel shortage
_C_ G. new ways to fight tooth decay
_S_ H. sharks
_S_ I. the benefits of regular exercise
_U_ J. reasons that advertising for alcohol should be banned
_A_ K. ways to solve traffic congestion in this city
_C_ L. space shuttles
_C_ M. the process of photosynthesis
_b_ N. how computers will change our homes in the future
_C_ O. methods of obtaining salt
_U_ P. a comparison of a computer and the human brain

3. When all the groups have finished, compare your results.

ACTIVITY 4-D

1. Write down two topics that you think would be suitable for a five- to ten-minute presentation to be given to the students in your class.
2. Give these topics to the instructor who will list some of them on the board or on handouts.
3. Now work in small groups. Decide whether each topic would be satisfactory or unsatisfactory as a five- to ten-minute presentation to be given to your class. In analyzing each topic, consider whether it is (a) too limited, (b) too general, (c) too technical, or (d) too well known for the students in your class. If the topic is unsatisfactory, indicate what the problem is. Can you revise the unsatisfactory topics to make them satisfactory?
4. When all the groups have finished, compare your results.

Presentation Techniques

CONCLUDING A PRESENTATION

The conclusion of your presentation is important because you want to leave a strong impression on your listeners. You should be brief and to the point in concluding your presentation. This is definitely not the time to introduce any new points. You want to remind listeners of what you have presented. To conclude a presentation you can:

- summarize or review the main points you have presented
- remind listeners of the importance of what you have said
- emphasize your major conclusions
- recommend further study of the subject
- ask the listeners to take appropriate action

You should not surprise people by suddenly announcing, "That's all," or "I guess I'm finished." That kind of ending shows that you have not organized your ideas very well. You should plan a conclusion to prepare the listeners for the end of your presentation. Here are some different ways to signal your listeners that you are concluding:

In $\left\{ \begin{array}{l} \text{conclusion,} \\ \text{closing,} \end{array} \right\}$ _____.

To $\left\{ \begin{array}{l} \text{conclude,} \\ \text{sum up,} \end{array} \right\}$ _____.

Before I end, let me quickly review the main points (advantages, reasons, effects, causes, types) of _____.

Briefly, then, I'd like to summarize the major points I've presented.

Before I open this up for your questions, I'd like to emphasize how important it is for you to remember _____.

You can end your presentation by asking listeners whether they have any questions. This allows people to ask for explanations or to get further information on a particular point.

ACTIVITY 4-E

1. Choose a problem in class, at work, in the community, or in the country where you live. Select a problem that you feel deserves

the special attention of the students in your class. Think of some ideas that you could include in a presentation on this topic.

2. Work individually to prepare a one- to two-minute conclusion to a presentation on this topic. Develop an effective conclusion that you feel will leave a strong impression on your listeners.

3. When everyone has finished, work in small groups. Take turns presenting your conclusions to the group. After each speaker has finished, discuss the strengths and weaknesses of the conclusion. Did the speaker include all of the elements of an effective conclusion?

Presentation Assignment 2

After studying the information in this unit, you can prepare a four- to five-minute presentation to give to a group or to the entire class. Look at the presentation evaluation form on page 68 to see how you will be evaluated. You can use the following guidelines to help you prepare your presentation:

1. Your instructor may assign a topic or allow you to choose your own. A list of suggested presentation assignments follows this list of guidelines, but you should choose a specific topic based on your knowledge and experience. If possible, your topic should relate to your major or field of specialization. To help you think of different possible ideas, you can fill out Worksheet 1 on page 241 of Appendix I.

2. In order to choose a specific topic that will be interesting or useful to your listeners, analyze your audience carefully. Fill out a copy of Worksheet 2 on page 246 of Appendix I.

3. Review the ideas you brainstormed earlier. After considering the characteristics of your listeners, try to select several topics that would be suitable for class presentations. Ask yourself these questions about each topic:
   A. Do you know enough about this topic?
   B. If some research is needed, do you have the time and re-sources to find the information?
   C. Have you limited the topic enough so that you can cover it adequately in the time available?
   D. Is the topic of potential interest to your listeners?
   E. Is the topic too difficult or too technical for this audience?
   F. Is the topic too easy or too well-known to this audience?

4. Fill out a copy of Worksheet 3 on page 249 of Appendix I to turn in to your instructor. Consider any suggestions from your instructor

before you make the final selection of the topic for your presentation.

5. Once you have chosen your topic and thought about how to organize your information, gather the information you want to include in your presentation. If you wish, you may do some additional research on your topic.

6. Make an outline of the points you want to present. Do not write out every word of your presentation. Check the outline to make sure that you have put your points in a logical order.

7. Plan your introduction and conclusion.

8. Review your outline until you know the material very well. Do not, however, try to memorize all of the information.

9. Since this is an extemporaneous presentation, you can write very brief notes on small note cards to help you remember the order of the main points that you want to present.

10. Before giving your presentation, check with the instructor or a dictionary about the correct pronunciation of any new or unfamiliar vocabulary words.

11. If you wish, prepare a short list of any specialized or technical terms that you are going to use in your presentation. Make sure that you know how to explain these to your listeners in clear, simple English. You may want to write these words on the blackboard at the beginning of your presentation.

12. Using your notes, practice giving your presentation several times before you have to give it in class. During practice make sure that your presentation meets the time requirements of the assignment.

Suggested Topics

1. Instruct or demonstrate to the listeners how to do or make something.

   Sample topics:
   > how to apply for a research grant
   > how to grow herbs at home
   > how to install an electrical outlet
   > how to build a bird feeder
   > how to improve fire safety in your home
   > how to get a good night's sleep
   > how to improve your memory
   > how to set up an aquarium
   > how to lower your electricity bills
   > how to control your blood pressure

Guidelines:

A. Give clear instructions so that the listeners will be able to follow and repeat the steps you are explaining.
B. Put the steps in the correct order.
C. Be sure not to leave out any necessary step.
D. Include any necessary precautions that the listeners should be aware of.
E. A visual aid, if practical, will help listeners follow your instructions.

2. Demonstrate to the class how to conduct a simple experiment.

Guidelines:

A. Choose a short experiment that is possible to do in front of the class.
B. Be sure to bring all of the necessary equipment with you to class.
C. The presentation should include:
   - the purpose of the experiment
   - necessary background information
   - warnings of possible dangers
   - a clear explanation of each step
   - an explanation of the results
   - an analysis of the results

3. Explain a process that your listeners can understand, but one that they probably do not already know.

Sample topics:

   how sedimentary rock is formed
   how glass is made
   how a star is formed
   how petroleum is refined
   how a volcano is formed
   how paper is manufactured
   how food is turned into energy
   how satellite television functions
   how plants are grafted
   how clouds are seeded

Guidelines:

A. The presentation should include:
   - an explanation of exactly what the process is
   - a description of the basic apparatus
   - an explanation of the theory or principle involved
   - a step-by-step description of the process
B. Do not go into so much detail that the listeners are confused.

C. A visual aid such as a drawing or a diagram may help your listeners understand the process more easily.

4. Explain how something was discovered, invented, or developed.

Sample topics:

how enzymes were discovered
how the cure for scurvy was discovered
how the radio (television, telephone) was invented
how the pyramids were built
how small pox was eradicated
how radium (radioactivity, the structure of DNA) was discovered
how instant cameras were developed
how motion pictures were developed
how the laws of heredity were discovered
how the first computer was invented

5. Summarize an article from a professional journal in your field.

Guidelines:

A. Include the title, date, author(s), and source of the article in the introduction.
B. Be sure to express the author's message accurately.
C. Put the summary into your own words.
D. Include all of the main points covered in the original article:
   • statement of the problem or issue
   • review of the relevant research
   • description of the research design and method
   • significant research results
   • analysis of the results
E. Leave out minor supporting details such as complicated explanations, long examples, complex statistics.
F. Do not include your personal comments.
G. Follow the order of the original, but add transitions to emphasize the relationship of the ideas.
H. Do not make the summary too technical.

6. Summarize a formal written report you have prepared for work or for a course.

Guidelines: See guidelines listed in #5.

7. Summarize an article on a scientific or technical subject from a popular or general magazine.

Guidelines: See guidelines listed in #5.

8. Summarize a lecture you have attended on a subject of interest. Make sure that you have accurate notes of the significant points covered during the lecture.

Guidelines: See guidelines listed in #5.

Suggested Assignments for Listeners

The instructor may assign different students to do some of the following listening assignments. The listeners should then turn in their assignments to the instructor, give them to the speaker, or discuss their results with the rest of the group or class, according to the teacher's instructions.

1. Fill out the evaluation form.
2. Write two questions to ask the speaker about the presentation.
3. Pay particular attention to the conclusion. Consider the following questions in analyzing the strengths and weaknesses of the conclusion:
   A. Was the conclusion well-prepared?
   B. What expression did the speaker use to lead into the conclusion?
   C. Exactly how did the speaker conclude: by summarizing the main points, by making a recommendation, by asking for action?
   D. Did the speaker ask for questions from the audience?
   E. Can you offer any suggestions for improving the conclusion?
4. Pay particular attention to the content of the presentation. Consider the following questions in analyzing the strengths and weaknesses of the content:
   A. What kinds of details, examples, or facts did the speaker include that related to the interests of this particular audience?
   B. Did the speaker use appropriate vocabulary for the language level of the listeners?
   C. What level of technical understanding did the speaker address: expert, technically informed, nontechnical, or mixed? Was it at the right level for these particular listeners?
   D. Did the speaker build on the existing knowledge of the listeners? Was the information too simple or too complex for this audience?
   E. Did the presentation meet the time requirements?

Presentation Evaluation 2

Speaker: _____

Topic: _____

Evaluator: _____

Rating System
Complete the following evaluation form by filling in the appropriate number of points in the blanks provided. The point values are as follows:

2 = Excellent   1 = Satisfactory   0 = Needs Improvement

These points can be added up to give a total score for each section of the form. Follow your teacher's instructions in rating the speaker on one or both of the sections included in this form. Space is provided for your comments on specific strengths or weaknesses of the speaker's presentation. You can also add suggestions for improving future presentations.

I. *Delivery*

Points out of 10: _____   *Comments:*

_____ A. volume—loud enough
to be heard clearly
_____ B. eye contact with audience
_____ C. natural delivery—not
read or memorized
_____ D. rate of speech—not too
fast or too slow
_____ E. posture/body movement—no distracting
mannerisms

II. *Content*

Points out of 10: _____   *Comments:*

_____ A. clear central idea
_____ B. topic suitable for time
available—not too limited
or too general

_____ C. topic suitable for this audience—not too technical or too well-known

_____ D. topic developed with relevant details, facts, examples that provide strong support of central idea

_____ E. presentation meets time requirements—not too long or too short

Total Number of Points Received by Speaker: _____

Total Number of Possible Points: _____

Questions to ask the speaker:

1. _____

2. _____

Examining Ideas

Expressions

The following list includes only some of the many possible expressions that are used to convey each function. Space is provided for you to add other expressions related to each function as you work through the unit. Before going over the lists provided, you may want to discuss each function and then work individually or in small groups to list expressions that you are already familiar with. You can identify any expressions that seem to be particularly formal, informal, direct, or indirect and then compare them with those listed here. You might also discuss possible situations in which these expressions could appropriately be used.

Asking for information

Who _____?	Why _____?
Which _____?	How _____?
What _____?	How often _____?
What kind of _____?	How much _____?
Where _____?	How many _____?
When _____?	How long _____?

Asking about support

What do you think of _____?
How do you feel about _____?
Are you in favor of _____?

Supporting an idea

I think _____ is $\left\{\begin{array}{l}\text{a good}\\\text{an excellent}\end{array}\right\}$ $\left\{\begin{array}{l}\text{idea}\\\text{suggestion}\\\text{plan}\end{array}\right\}$

because _____ .

$\left.\begin{array}{l}\text{I'm for}\\\text{I'm in favor of}\\\text{I support}\end{array}\right\}$ _____ because _____ .

The main advantage of _____ is that _____ .

Opposing an idea

I think _____ isn't a good idea because _____ .

$\left.\begin{array}{l}\text{I'm against}\\\text{I'm not in favor of}\end{array}\right\}$ _____ because _____ .

The main disadvantage of _____ is that _____ .

Listening Practice

The following exercises can be completed by listening to Unit 5 on the tape.

Section 1.   There are twelve questions in this section. They are part of a conversation between a health-care worker and a patient. The health-care worker is taking the patient's medical history.

A.   Before listening to the tape, work individually, with a partner, or in a small group to brainstorm possible questions that a health-care worker might ask a patient in order to obtain a brief medical history. List these questions on a separate sheet of paper.

B.   Now listen to Section 1 on the tape. For each question choose an appropriate answer from the choices given. Circle the letter of that answer.

1. a. Five months.
   b. Thirty.
   c. 1960.

2. a. I have a pain in my chest.
   b. Fine, thank you.
   c. I'm waiting to see the doctor.

3. a. Very strong.
   b. A month.
   c. Twice a day.

4. a. At the hospital.
   b. Once.
   c. Two weeks ago.

5. a. Yes, pain pills.
    b. Yes, from the pharmacy.
    c. Yes, a headache.

6. a. Eight.
    b. Three times a day.
    c. One week.

7. a. After I eat.
    b. Four times a day.
    c. With a glass of water.

8. a. Yes, a heart attack.
    b. Yes, for ten years.
    c. Yes, my father.

9. a. Yes, I think I need one.
    b. Yes, my family doctor.
    c. Yes, I had my appendix out.

10. a. Ten years ago.
    b. For a month.
    c. In a week.

11. a. In 1975.
    b. Two weeks.
    c. Last January.

12. a. No, I haven't.
    b. No, I won't.
    c. No, I'm not.

C. Work with a partner, in a small group, or as a class to compare your answers. How many questions on your list were included on the tape?

Section 2. There are eight short dialogs in this section. Each one is about a different subject.

A. Listen to Section 2 on the tape. For each dialog complete the statement concerning what the first speaker said. Circle the letter of the correct answer.

1. The woman wants to put in a _____.
   a. stop sign   b. traffic light

2. The man wants to pay _____ for electricity.
   a. more   b. less

3. The woman mentions a plan to _____ hunting on public property.
   a. prohibit   b. allow

4. _____ will be immunized against influenza.
   a. Everyone   b. The elderly

5. The woman wants to control the infestation _____.
   a. naturally   b. chemically

6. The man wants to launch two satellites _____.
   a. within twelve months.   b. immediately.

7. The woman wants to _____ the experiment.
   a. continue   b. halt

8. The man _____ to send food to help the people suffering from the drought.
   a. wants   b. doesn't want

B. Work with a partner, in a small group, or as a class to compare your answers.

C. Listen again. Does the second speaker support or oppose the idea of the first speaker? Put a check [✔] in the correct space.

Support Oppose   Expressions

1. _____ _____   _____

2. _____ _____   _____

3. _____ _____   _____

4. _____ _____   _____

5. _____ _____   _____

6. _____ _____   _____

7. _____ _____   _____

8. _____ _____   _____

D. Listen a third time. Write the expression the speaker uses to support or oppose each idea in the list above.

E. Work with a partner, in a small group, or as a class to compare your answers.

Controlled Practice

Exercise 1. Look at the photographs on page 75. Do you know what is happening in these pictures? What kind of questions do you need to ask in order to learn as much as possible about the situation?

> *Student A:* Ask questions to find out more about the situation you see in the picture.
>
> *Student B:* Answer the questions with reasonable responses.

Exercise 2.   The following exercises are brief statements that do not include complete information about a situation. Ask a variety of questions to find out more details about the situation.

> *Student A:*   Ask a question about the situation.
>
> *Student B:*   Answer the question with any reasonable response.
>
> *Student A:*   Ask another question.
>
> *Student B:*   Answer with any reasonable response.

1. *Sign on photocopier:* MACHINE OUT OF ORDER.
2. *Problem:* Students have complaints about the class.
3. *Rumor:* Two people were fired from the company.
4. *Sign on classroom blackboard:* CLASS CANCELLED.
5. *Problem:* Many trees in a park are dying.
6. *Advice:* The company should buy a new computer system.
7. *Problem:* The patient's temperature is above normal.
8. *Newspaper headline:* 150 PEOPLE DIE IN AIR DISASTER.
9. *Problem:* Much lab equipment has been disappearing lately.
10. *Rumor:* The company might be opening a new factory in another country.
11. *Newspaper headline:* BRIDGE COLLAPSES!
12. *Advice:* The company should manufacture a new product.
13. *Problem:* Parents are not having their children vaccinated.
14. *Rumor:* All high school students in the nation will be required to study physics.
15. *Newspaper headline:* LOCAL SCIENTIST WINS NOBEL PRIZE.
16. *Problem:* Many outstanding scientists are leaving universities to work in industry.
17. *Advice:* The city should build a new zoo.
18. *Newspaper headline:* NEW TREATMENT FOR CANCER.
19. *Problem:* Road accidents are increasing.
20. *Advertisement in newspaper:* COMPUTER SALE!

What's Going on Here?

Who?   Which?   What?   What kind of?   Where?   When?   Why?
How long?   How often?   How much?   How many?

1. an oil spill

2. a flood

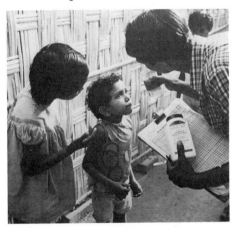

3. a community health program

4. a crowded clinic

Exercise 3. Be sure that you understand all of the following terms before going over this exercise in class. Use a variety of expressions from the unit.

> *Student A:* Ask Student B's opinion on one of the following.
>
> *Student B:* Support the idea and explain one advantage *or* oppose the idea and give a disadvantage.

General Interest

1. drilling for oil in the Antarctic
2. solar energy
3. increasing the pay of high school science teachers
4. sending teenage drug abusers to prison
5. experimenting on dogs
6. banning video games in public places
7. increasing the budget for space exploration
8. banning smoking in all public places
9. nuclear weapons
10. asking job applicants to take lie-detector tests

Science

11. using chemical pesticides
12. zero population growth
13. irradiating food to preserve it
14. genetic engineering
15. the "save the whales" campaign

Engineering

16. battery-powered cars
17. banning billboards along all highways
18. strict emission controls on automobiles
19. building six-lane highways through cities
20. increasing the number of supersonic airplanes

Health

21. daily vitamin supplements
22. surrogate mothers
23. adding fluoride to a city's water supply
24. artificial hearts
25. hypnosis as anesthesia

Communication Concepts

EFFECTIVE LEADERSHIP

If you are the leader of a discussion group, it is your responsibility to begin and end the meeting on time. There are also other responsibilities that you need to fulfill in order to be an effective leader:

1. Prepare an agenda for the meeting to give to the participants in advance, if possible. Since the agenda lists the order of the main points to be discussed, it will help guide the discussion.
2. If there is only one issue to discuss, you may feel that an agenda is not necessary. In this case, be sure to make the purpose or goal of the meeting clear.
3. See that all group members have an equal chance to participate. Bring in quiet participants by asking them questions. Also, control people who talk too much or monopolize the discussion.
4. Keep the discussion on the subject. If participants start moving off the topic or bringing up irrelevant points, politely bring the discussion back to the subject.
5. Keep the discussion moving. You have to cut off conversation if members spend too much time on one point or start repeating the same ideas. However, you also have to decide when conversation is useful and should be encouraged.
6. Try to keep the discussion organized. Once a suggestion has been introduced, try to get the group to examine it thoroughly before moving on to the next point.
7. Summarize when needed and look for areas of agreement. Of course, you are looking for agreement, but you cannot force it.
8. Make sure that all participants understand the discussion. In order to do this, you may have to restate or explain certain points.
9. Be fair and objective in considering all opinions that are expressed. Since a leader's opinion can have a strong effect on the participants, try not to be too forceful in stating your own opinions. One way to do this is by putting your ideas in the form of questions or suggestions. For example, you can ask "What do you think about _____?" or "What about _____?"
10. At the end of the meeting summarize the group's decision. Make sure that all participants understand and accept this decision.

Discussion Techniques

KEEPING COMMUNICATION OPEN

For effective interaction to take place in a discussion, all of the participants must be able to express their ideas. To encourage open communication, the leader or other group members should bring in people who are not actively participating in the discussion. A usual way
of bringing others into the discussion is by asking them questions:

What do you $\begin{cases} \text{think?} \\ \text{suggest?} \end{cases}$

What's your opinion of _____?

Do you have anything to add?

Furthermore, the leader may have to control a group member who is
talking too much:

Yes, I see what you mean, but let's see what some of the others
have to say about this.

I think you've got a good point there. Can we hear what some
others think about this?

Discussion Practice

ANALYZING A PROBLEM

The cases in this section are designed to give you practice in analyzing a problem. Each case provides you with a problem to analyze in a
small group as part of a discussion role play.

In many discussion role plays, the goal of the discussion is to
find the most effective solution to a particular problem. The problem
to be solved is clearly defined and described in the situation. In a real-
life situation, however, a problem is not always so easy to determine.
You may need to spend some time investigating a situation in order to
develop a clear definition of the problem. It is essential for you to
identify all of the different factors involved in the problem before beginning to look for a solution. In order to analyze a problem you need
to find out: (a) the facts of the situation, (b) the extent of the problem

(how serious or harmful it is), (c) the history or background, (d) the causes, and (e) the effects of the problem. You can find the answers to these questions by asking specific "who, which, what, what kind of, where, when, why, how, how often, how much, how many, and how long" questions about the situation.

Instructions

1. Work in small groups. All groups may be assigned to work on the same case in order to compare results, or groups may work on different cases according to their particular interests.
2. Choose a group leader. Work together to develop specific questions about the problem described in the situation. Of course, you will not know the answers to the questions. Your purpose is to list questions that would be useful in analyzing the problem. An example is provided to show you possible questions used to analyze one particular situation.
3. After developing a long list of possible questions, consider the following:
   A. Are any of the questions irrelevant or unnecessary?
   B. Do any of the questions repeat others?
   C. Are all of the questions clear and concise?
   D. Are all of the questions grammatically correct?
   E. Should any other important questions be added?
4. Revise the list of questions until you are all satisfied with it. One person in the group can write out a final list of the questions you have developed. Include the names of all group members on this list.
5. If other groups have worked on the same case, compare lists of questions. How many similar questions did the groups develop? After comparing ideas, you may want to revise your list.
6. After you have finished, turn in your list of questions to the instructor and complete the Participant Evaluation Form on page 83.

EXAMPLE PROBLEM ANALYSIS

Executives of a manufacturing company are holding a meeting to discuss an increase in the rate of absenteeism. Make a list of questions the executives should consider in analyzing the problem before they can begin to consider any possible solutions.

1. Who has identified absenteeism as a problem?
2. What is the current rate of absenteeism?
3. What kind of absentee rate have we had in the past?
4. What is considered to be an acceptable rate of absenteeism?
5. What is the history of this problem? That is, have we had such a high rate in the past? What action was taken to solve the problem? Was this action effective?
6. Does the absentee rate usually increase during certain times of the year?
7. Is the absentee rate about the same in all departments or divisions of the company?
8. Is the absentee rate about the same for different categories of workers: executives, foremen, assembly line workers, skilled technicians, secretarial staff?
9. Is there a pattern to the days that workers are absent? That is, are they usually absent on the day before or the day following a weekend?
10. Are certain workers frequently absent, or are many workers occasionally absent?
11. Are the absences generally for one day, several days, or more?
12. What effects does this high rate of absenteeism have on production?
13. What other effects does this absenteeism have on the company?
14. What are some possible causes of this problem?
15. What seem to be the major causes of the problem?

The following cases provide a variety of problems for you to analyze:

CASE 1: IN-SERVICE TRAINING COURSE

Situation

A company regularly offers in-service training courses in oral communication skills to science professionals in the company. With still half of the course to complete, more than 50 percent of the students have dropped out of the current course. Make a list of questions that company officials should ask before beginning to consider possible courses of action.

CASE 2: BUILDING COLLAPSE

Situation

Last week a five-year-old apartment building in the downtown area collapsed, killing several people. A government agency has been asked to conduct a complete investigation of the disaster. Make a list of questions that the agency officials should ask before beginning to consider possible courses of action.

CASE 3: FOOD POISONING

Situation

More than 60 percent of the people attending a convention have come down with serious cases of food poisoning. Make a list of questions that health officials should ask before beginning to consider possible courses of action.

CASE 4: DYING ANIMALS

Situation

A laboratory technician has reported that many laboratory animals have been dying recently of unknown causes. Make a list of questions that the head of the laboratory should ask before beginning to consider possible courses of action.

CASE 5: FEWER TRAIN PASSENGERS

Situation

The National Rail Service has reported huge losses of revenue due to declining numbers of passengers. Make a list of questions that government officials should ask before beginning to consider possible courses of action.

CASE 6: DEFECTIVE PRODUCTS

Situation

The manager of a factory is faced with the problem of increasing numbers of defective products being manufactured in the plant. Make a list of questions that the manager should ask before beginning to consider possible courses of action.

CASE 7: YOUR OWN PROBLEM

Situation

Choose a problem in class, in your university, in the company you work for, in your community, or in your country. Make a list of questions that you should ask before beginning to consider possible solutions to this problem.

Discussion Evaluation

PARTICIPANT EVALUATION FORM

1. *Identifying the group*

   A. Discussion topic: _____

   B. Names of other students in your group: _____

   _____

2. *Rating your own discussion.* Use the following scales to rate your own discussion group:

   A. *Participation.* Did all group members interact and take equal part in the discussion?

Excellent	Satisfactory	Weak	Unsatisfactory
3	2	1	0

   B. *Clarity.* Did all of the group members speak loudly and clearly?

Excellent	Satisfactory	Weak	Unsatisfactory
3	2	1	0

   C. *Pace.* Did the discussion move along at the right speed, without long pauses between speakers?

Excellent	Satisfactory	Weak	Unsatisfactory
3	2	1	0

   D. *Leader Control.* Did the leader effectively guide the discussion, not taking too much or too little control?

Excellent	Satisfactory	Weak	Unsatisfactory
3	2	1	0

3. *Making suggestions.* What suggestions can you make to improve your next group discussion?

_____

_____

_____

_____

Dealing with Facts

Expressions

The following list includes only some of the many possible expressions that are used to convey each function. Space is provided for you to add other expressions related to each function as you work through the unit. Before going over the lists provided, you may want to discuss each function and then work individually or in small groups to list expressions that you are already familiar with. You can identify any expressions that seem to be particularly formal, informal, direct, or indirect and then compare them with those listed here. You might also discuss possible situations in which these expressions could appropriately be used.

> *Stating a fact*
> Everyone knows that _____.
> It's a fact that _____.

> *Note*: In most cases there are no special expressions to introduce a statement of fact. A fact is a statement about reality that can be proved or verified as true. The following are examples of facts:
>
> Alexander Bell invented the telephone.
> A plant is a living organism.
> In general, warm air rises and cool air sinks.
> Silicon chips are used in calculators and computers.

Refuting
   Actually, _____.
   In fact, _____.
   As a matter of fact, _____.
   Well, I'm not really sure that's correct.
   Are you sure that's right? Isn't it true that _____?

Asking for examples
   For example?
   For instance?
   Such as?
   Could you give me an example?

Giving examples
   Let me give you an example.
   To give you an example, _____.
   For example, _____.
   For instance, _____.

Listening Practice

The following exercises can be completed by listening to Unit 6 on the tape.

Section 1. There are ten short dialogs in this section. Each dialog is about a different subject.

A. Listen to Section 1 on the tape. Decide whether the speakers are discussing a fact or an opinion in each dialog. Put a check [✓] in the correct space.

	Fact	Opinion	General Subject
1.	_____	_____	_____
2.	_____	_____	_____
3.	_____	_____	_____
4.	_____	_____	_____

Fact   *Opinion*   *General Subject*

5. _____ _____   _____

6. _____ _____   _____

7. _____ _____   _____

8. _____ _____   _____

9. _____ _____   _____

10. _____ _____   _____

B. Listen again. In a few words write the general subject of each dialog.

C. Work with a partner, in a small group, or as a class to compare your answers.

Section 2. There are five separate dialogs in this section. They are all between a student and a professor.

A. Listen to Section 2 on the tape. Write the expression each speaker uses to refute the following statements.

Statements	*Expressions*
1. Undergraduates are never hired as lab assistants.	_____
2. The student needs only the professor's signature to take Industrial Electronics.	_____
3. The university will never recognize research unless it is done in university labs.	_____
4. The student has missed three lab classes.	_____
5. Both required courses meet at the same time.	_____

B. Work with a partner, in a small group, or as a class to compare your answers.

Controlled Practice

Exercise 1.   Look at the charts on pages 89 and 90. Some of the information in these charts is correct and some of the information is incorrect. Use a variety of expressions from the unit in discussing these charts. All students should try to fill in the blank charts with the correct information.

Student A: Ask a question in order to fill in the blank chart.

Student B: Answer the question according to the information provided in the chart (whether it is correct or incorrect).

Student C: If the information is incorrect, refute the statement and give the correct information.

Exercise 2.   All the following statements are incorrect. In doing this exercise, use a variety of expressions from the unit to refute each statement.

Student A: Say the statement.

Student B: Refute the statement and then give the correct information.

General Interest

1. Microwaves are very long radio waves.
2. Oxygen is liquid at room temperature.
3. Morse code is a system that allows blind people to read.
4. Computer software is the physical equipment that makes up a computer system.
5. Pure water boils at 212 degrees centigrade at normal atmospheric pressure.
6. A barometer is an instrument for measuring temperature.
7. Wood is an example of a fossil fuel.
8. It takes the earth one month to travel around the sun.
9. The surface of a star is very cold.

Science

11. Spiders have six legs.
12. Mammals are coldblooded vertebrates.
13. Hydrogen is needed for photosynthesis.

Can This Be Right?

Classifying Vertebrate Animals

Mammals

tiger

penguin

owl

Reptiles

turtle

rabbit

whale

Amphibians

lizard

crocodile

frog

Birds

bat

robin

chicken

Can This Be Right?

Classifying Vertebrate Animals

Fill in the following chart with the correct information:

Mammals	*Amphibians*	*Reptiles*	*Birds*

Chemical Symbols

Metals

aluminum	Al	magnesium	Ma
calcium	Ca	potassium	K
copper	Co	silver	Si
gold	Ag	sodium	So
iron	Ir	tin	Sn
lead	Pb	zinc	Zn

Fill in the following chart with the correct chemical symbols:

Metals

aluminum	_____	magnesium	_____
calcium	_____	potassium	_____
copper	_____	silver	_____
gold	_____	sodium	_____
iron	_____	tin	_____
lead	_____	zinc	_____

14. In an atom protons orbit around a nucleus of electrons.
15. Red litmus paper indicates that a solution is alkaline.

Engineering

16. Copper is an alloy.
17. A cathode is the positive terminal in an electrolytic cell.
18. An alternator is a device which changes an AC voltage to a higher or lower AC voltage.
19. The carburetor of an engine supplies the cylinder with water and gas mixed in the right proportions.
20. Rubber is a good conductor of heat.

Health

21. Blood leaves the heart through the veins.
22. The common cold is caused by bacteria.
23. Knees and elbows are muscles.
24. Alexander Fleming is famous for his discovery of viruses.
25. The body breaks down carbohydrates into amino acids.

Exercise 3. Use a variety of expressions from the unit.

> *Student A:* Make a general statement about each of the following points, such as "There are many [several] different _____."
>
> *Student B:* Ask for examples.
>
> *Student A:* Give a few examples.

General Interest

1. planets
2. elements
3. sports to improve physical fitness
4. scientific journals
5. uses of radiation
6. fossil fuels
7. types of natural disasters
8. uses of lasers
9. metals
10. computer languages

Science

11. uses of salt
12. ways to stop the growth of bacteria

13. acids
14. vitamins
15. parts of a cell

Engineering

16. types of engines
17. good conductors of heat
18. types of batteries
19. areas of specialization in engineering
20. types of waves

Health

21. medical specialties
22. organs in the body
23. duties of a nurse
24. functions of the blood
25. joints in the body

Communication Concepts

EFFECTIVE PARTICIPATION

In order for you to be an effective participant in a group discussion, you should keep in mind the following points:

1. Speak loudly and clearly enough for everyone to hear you. Also, use words that you know the others will understand, or be ready to explain the meanings of any new or difficult words that you use.
2. Understand the goal of the discussion and be sure to keep all of your comments and questions on the subject.
3. Be prepared for the discussion. Study or collect all of the information you need in order to participate actively in the discussion.
4. Show initiative in the discussion. Do not wait for others to ask you questions before you make your comments. It is your responsibility to participate.
5. Listen carefully to the other participants' ideas so that you can interact with them. You should examine their ideas by asking questions, getting further information, agreeing, and disagreeing. Be sure to ask questions if you do not understand what is going on.

6. Present your ideas as concisely as possible. This means that your comments should be brief and to the point. It is usually more effective to make several brief remarks rather than one long statement.

7. If you have several important points to make, do not try to explain them all at once. The other members of the group will not be able to remember everything you have said. Thus, some of your points may be lost or ignored. It is better to make one strong point which the others can respond to. You can then present your other ideas at appropriate points in the discussion.

8. Work as a member of a team. Present your ideas, but also bring in group members who are quiet or shy. You must be willing to share speaking time and to consider opinions that are different from yours.

9. Be prepared to support your opinions with facts, reasons, and examples. Do not change your mind just because someone disagrees with you. Explain why you feel the way you do. Remember that a conflict of ideas within a group is useful since it helps the group to see different sides of an issue.

10. Keep an open mind. Once you have supported your opinion, be prepared to compromise or to change your position if others present strong arguments.

Discussion Techniques

INTERRUPTING

Interrupting is a technique that should not be used very often since you want to let others finish their turn at speaking. Some speakers may speak quite slowly, but you have to be patient and allow them time to get their thoughts out. However, there are times when interrupting is appropriate. For example, if someone has been talking for some time, you may feel that you must get a point in. In this case, you can wait for a natural pause in the flow of speech—such as at the end of a sentence—and then say:

Excuse me, _____.

Excuse
Pardon } me for interrupting, but _____.

Sorry to interrupt, but _____.

Of course, it is possible that someone may try to interrupt you before you have finished speaking. Then you can try to prevent that person from interrupting you by saying in a polite way:

Just a $\left\{\begin{array}{l}\text{moment,}\\\text{minute,}\end{array}\right\}$ please. Let me just finish this point.

Excuse me. Could I just finish my point?

I'm not quite finished. Just a second.

If you could wait a moment, I'm almost finished.

Discussion Practice

SOLVING A PROBLEM

The cases in this section will give you further practice in participating in problem-solving discussions.

Instructions

1. Refer to the detailed instructions included in the Discussion Practice section of Unit 2 for guidance in choosing cases, getting organized, brainstorming, selecting ideas, preparing for, and starting the discussion. In your discussion the group leader should try to keep the group moving toward the goal in an organized way.
2. Group observers should complete the Observer Evaluation Form on page 98 as directed by the instructor. They can then discuss their evaluations with the group members. If other groups have worked on the same case, compare your solutions.

CASE 1: KNOWLEDGE OF BASIC TECHNOLOGIES

Situation

The National Science Foundation (NSF) has recently published a surprising report. Studies show that in this highly developed country only one in five people understands what radiation is and even fewer understand how a telephone works. People seem to have a blind belief in science without really understanding it. NSF officials are very concerned about this because many important issues of today require knowledge of technology. They feel that the country cannot afford to have citizens who do not understand even the basics of science. The NSF has asked for a general meeting to discuss this issue.

Purpose of the Discussion

Group members should try to agree on the best way to improve the level of technical knowledge among the general public.

Group Roles

The following people take part in the discussion:

> Leader: a representative of the government
> Representative(s) of the National Science Foundation
> Citizen(s)

CASE 2: A LANGUAGE POLICY

Situation

Consultants have been called in to evaluate the quality of the College of Science and Technology in a university. Currently all science courses are taught in the students' native language, and English is taught as a foreign language. The consultants have recommended that the college be changed to an English-language institution because English is the international language of science and technology. Administrators question the practicality of the recommendation. They say that it will require a restructuring of the entire educational system. Most students are not prepared to undertake a university program in English. Faculty members are opposed to the idea. They feel that it is an unnecessary requirement. Furthermore, they say that such a measure will reduce the number of graduates, a possibility the country cannot afford. A meeting has been called to discuss the issue.

Purpose of the Discussion

Group members should try to agree on the best language policy for the College of Science and Technology.

Group Roles

The following people take part in the discussion:

> Leader: an administrator of the university
> Consultant(s) evaluating the university
> Representative(s) of the faculty
> Representative(s) of the students

CASE 3: AN ENERGY POLICY

Situation

A nuclear power plant in an industrialized country has been forced to close for several weeks because of radiation leaks. This latest accident has added to the controversy surrounding the building of a second nuclear plant. Citizens opposed to nuclear energy want to stop construction at the new site. They believe that nuclear energy is too dangerous. Members of the Industrial Development Organization (IDO), however, want construction on the new plant to continue. They say that all methods of power generation involve some risks. Traditional methods, for example, can cause gaseous and particulate pollution. The IDO further maintains that nuclear power should not be dismissed because of potentially hazardous situations that are unlikely to occur. The organization also says that nuclear energy is much more economical and cleaner than other forms of energy. A meeting has been called to discuss the situation.

Purpose of the Discussion

Group members should try to agree on the best energy policy for this country.

Group Roles

The following people take part in the discussion:

> Leader: a representative of the government
> Citizen(s) opposed to nuclear energy
> Representative(s) of the Industrial Development Organization

CASE 4: SALE OF ANTIBIOTICS

Situation

A group of health professionals has suggested that all antibiotics, including penicillin, be sold only by prescription. Currently, in this developing country these drugs are sold without prescription as over-the-counter medicine. Health professionals believe that the present system of self-treatment delays proper treatment and has serious harmful effects. Citizens, however, are opposed to the health professionals' plan. They say that clinics are already overcrowded, and they do not want to waste time going to a doctor. Besides, an average worker often cannot afford to pay to see a doctor for a prescription and also pay for the medicine. A meeting has been called to discuss this issue.

Purpose of the Discussion

Group members should try to agree on the best policy regarding the sale of antibiotics in this country.

Group Roles

The following people take part in this discussion:

> Leader: a representative of the government
> Health professional(s)
> Citizen(s)

Discussion Evaluation

OBSERVER EVALUATION FORM

1. *Listening to an individual.* In this discussion you should observe only one speaker.

   A. Speaker's name/role: _____

   B. Discussion topic: _____

2. *Listening for functions and expressions.* Every time the person speaks during the discussion, make a note of the function he or she is using: (a) giving an opinion/making a statement, (b) suggesting, (c) agreeing/supporting, (d) disagreeing/opposing, (e) asking a question, (f) giving an example, (g) other. Before listening to the discussion, you may want to review the expressions that are associated with each of these functions. You can use the following chart to take notes on the discussion:

Expressions	*Functions*

3. *Rating the speaker.* Use the following scales to rate the speaker:

   A. *Interaction.* Did the speaker effectively interact with others? Use a variety of functions? Initiate? Involve others? Ask questions?

Excellent	Satisfactory	Weak	Unsatisfactory
3	2	1	0

   |_____|_____|_____|_____

B. *Use of Expressions.* Did the speaker effectively and accurately use a variety of expressions?

Excellent	Satisfactory	Weak	Unsatisfactory
3	2	1	0

4. *Making suggestions.* What suggestions can you give this speaker to help him or her improve?

_____

_____

_____

_____

Organizing Information

Presentation Preparation

ORGANIZING THE INFORMATION

A. Determining the Central Idea

When planning an informative presentation, you need to develop a clear statement of your central idea. This central idea is the main point you are trying to make in your presentation. It explains exactly what aspect of your topic you intend to cover. For example, you might want to choose robots as your subject. The topic of robots can be developed in a variety of ways. Your central idea might be (a) to explain the five types of arm robots, (b) to discuss the problems of using robots in a factory, (c) to analyze the advantages of using robots in a factory, (d) to describe the electric motor that drives a robot, (e) to explain how a robot recognizes things, or (f) to compare assembly lines using humans and those using robots. As you can see, the central idea states exactly what you intend to present in your presentation. Thus, it controls what you include in your presentation and also helps determine the arrangement of the main points.

ACTIVITY 7-A

1. Work in small groups. Develop several different speaking topics, each with a clear, central purpose, based on the general subjects listed below.
   A. computers
   B. AIDS
   C. dolphins
   D. rain forests
   E. skyscrapers
2. When all the groups have finished, compare your topics and select those that sound the most interesting.

B. Arranging the Main Points

Once you have a clear statement of your central idea, you can start developing the body, or main section, of your presentation. The body consists of main points that develop your central idea in detail. These main points need to be arranged in a way that is clear both to you and to your audience. The organization of your presentation should make it easy for the audience to understand and to remember the information you present. You need to select a pattern of organization that will work best with your particular topic. Here are some of the most commonly used patterns of organization along with skeleton outlines of sample topics:

Topical order. This common pattern divides the topic into smaller subtopics. Your central idea often determines the natural subtopics of your subject: benefits, disadvantages, uses, types, categories, ways, or reasons. Other topics may fall into standardized subtopics or classifications such as the division of animals into vertebrates and invertebrates or matter into organic and inorganic. At other times you have to choose the logical divisions of a topic. For example, pollution is often divided into different types: air, water, noise. In addition, you might discuss the resources needed for a project by categorizing them into areas of personnel, equipment, and facilities. These subtopics are then presented in a logical order:

- from the least important to the most important
- from the most important to the least important
- from the simple to the complex
- from the general to the specific
- from the specific to the general
- from the known to the unknown

A. Central idea: to classify something into categories

   Body:

   I. First category
   II. Second category
   III. Third category
   IV. Fourth category

B. Central idea: to explain the reasons for a certain decision

   Body:

   I. Most important reason
   II. Next most important reason
   III. Least important reason

Chronological order. This organization pattern arranges points as they occur in time. You put events in the order that they occur. This pattern is commonly used in explaining processes or giving instructions.

A. Central idea: to discuss the progress of a project

   Body:

   I. Past
   II. Present
   III. Future

B. Central idea: to explain the steps of a procedure

   Body:

   I. First step
   II. Second step
   III. Third step
   IV. Fourth step
   V. Fifth step

Spatial order. In this pattern the points are arranged according to some logical arrangement in space, such as from east to west, from far to near, from left to right, from top to bottom, or from inside to outside. This pattern is often used in physical descriptions of objects and places.

A. Central idea: to describe a building

   Body:

   I. First floor
   II. Second floor

III. Third floor
IV. Fourth floor

B. Central idea: to give a physical description of an object
   Body:
      I. Top
     II. Middle
    III. Bottom

Problem-solution. You may follow several patterns in a problem-solution organization. First, you might analyze the problem in detail and then offer one or two possible solutions in the conclusion. Second, you can briefly state the problem and then give a detailed explanation of the solution(s). Third, you can explain the problem and then recommend the best solution.

A. Central idea: to explain a certain problem in detail
   Body:
       I. Definition of the problem
      II. Background of the problem
     III. Causes of the problem
     IV. Effects of the problem
      V. Solutions to the problem

B. Central idea: to discuss several possible solutions to a problem
   Body:
       I. Definition of the problem (causes and effects)
      II. Solution 1
     III. Solution 2
     IV. Solution 3
      V. Solution 4

C. Central idea: to recommend a specific solution to a problem
   Body:
       I. Definition of the problem (causes and effects)
      II. Explanation of the recommended solution
     III. Reasons that this is the best solution

Cause and effect. This pattern can be organized in two ways. In one pattern you give a detailed explanation of the causes of an event, mentioning the effects only briefly. In the other plan you emphasize the effects or results of the event.

A. Central idea: to explain the main causes of a situation

   Body:

   I.   Explanation of the situation (and its effects)
   II. First cause
   III. Second cause
   IV. Third cause
   V.   Fourth cause

B. Central idea: to explain the main effects of a situation

   Body:

   I.   Explanation of the situation (and its causes)
   II. First effect
   III. Second effect
   IV. Third effect

   Reasons for and against. In this pattern you present both sides of an issue, first discussing all of the details on one side of the question and then all of the details on the other side.

Central idea: to explain reasons both for and against a position

   Body:

   I. Reasons against
   II. Reasons for

   Comparison/contrast. There are two basic patterns to follow when you compare or contrast two things: one-other and point-by-point. In the one-other pattern you use the things to be compared as the basis of organization. You first discuss one of the things to be compared in detail and then you discuss the other thing in detail. To make the comparison clear using this pattern, you need to discuss the same details in the same order. While the one-other pattern gives a general picture of the comparison, the point-by-point pattern emphasizes specific details. In the point-by-point pattern you use the points of comparison (or criteria) as the basis of organization. You then compare the two things point by point.

A. Central idea: to compare two solutions to a problem

   Body (one-other pattern):

   I. Solution 1
       A. Cost
       B. Practicality
       C. Side effects

D. Disadvantages
E. Advantages

II. Solution 2
A. Cost
B. Practicality
C. Side effects
D. Disadvantages
E. Advantages

B. Central idea: to compare two solutions to a problem

Body (point-by-point pattern):

I. Cost
A. Solution 1
B. Solution 2

II. Practicality
A. Solution 1
B. Solution 2

III. Side effects
A. Solution 1
B. Solution 2

IV. Disadvantages
A. Solution 1
B. Solution 2

V. Advantages
A. Solution 1
B. Solution 2

ACTIVITY 7-B

1. Work in small groups. Decide which pattern of organization would work best with the following topics: (a) topical, (b) chronological, (c) spatial, (d) problem-solution, (e) cause and effect, (f) reasons for and against, or (g) comparison/contrast:

_____ A. a progress report on installing a new computer system in the country

_____ B. the benefits of a new company policy

_____ C. how sewage water is treated

_____ D. the types of rocks in the earth's crust

_____ E. a description of a blast furnace

_____ F. describing how a force pump operates

_____ G. how an eye and a camera are similar

_____ H. several solutions to the problem of drug abuse

_____ I. describing two photocopy machines made by different companies

_____ J. the structure of a flowering plant

_____ K. the advantages and disadvantages of nuclear power

_____ L. what happens when tuna fishing is restricted

_____ M. why productivity has decreased in a factory

_____ N. the functions of the liver

_____ O. an explanation of the problem of poor writing skills of scientists

_____ P. simple cell versus dry cell batteries

2. When all the groups have finished, compare your results.
3. The instructor might ask you to make skeleton outlines of some of these topics.

ACTIVITY 7-C

1. Work as a class to choose one general subject area to consider, such as space exploration, environmental protection, or health.
2. Work individually to develop this general subject into four different speaking topics, each with a clear, central idea. Each topic should require or suggest a different pattern of organization.
3. Now work in small groups. Combine your ideas to develop a master list of at least ten different topics, making sure that each one has a clear, central idea.
4. Agree on the best pattern of organization for each topic on your master list. Try to include topics on your master list that require a variety of patterns of organization. List the appropriate patterns on an answer sheet, not on the master list.
5. Exchange master lists with another group. With the members of your group, agree on the best pattern of organization for the topics on the other group's master list. Write your ideas on another answer sheet, not on their master list.
6. When both groups have finished, compare your answer sheets and reach a final agreement on the best method of organization for the topics on both master sheets.

Presentation Techniques

USING TRANSITIONS

Every presentation you give includes many different pieces of information: main points supported by details, facts, examples, explanations, and reasons. In order for your listeners to understand the presentation, you need to use transitions to show how these pieces of information fit together into a clear, logical pattern. Transitions are the words, phrases, or sentences that connect and show the relationship of your ideas. By linking your ideas, transitions help your listeners follow your progress as you move from one point to another or from one part of your presentation to another. Here are some commonly used transitions and the relationships they show:

- *To connect ideas between sentences and between parts of the presentation*

    Addition: in addition, also, furthermore, moreover, and, besides, another

    Example: for instance, for example, to illustrate, specifically, such as

    Explanation: in other words, that is, to put it another way

    Time: now, first, second, third, next, then, later, before, after, finally, at the same time

    Result: therefore, thus, consequently, as a result, for this reason, as a consequence

    Cause: because, because of, since, is caused by, resulted from, is due to

    Space: to the left, to the right, above, below, under, over, inside, outside, nearby, next to, adjacent to

    Contrast: even so, nevertheless, although, though, even though, while, despite, despite the fact that, in contrast, on the other hand, however, otherwise

    Comparison: in comparison, similarly, in the same way, like, is like, can be compared to

    Generalization: in general, in most cases, usually, for the most part

    Reference: as I said earlier, as I mentioned before, to repeat what I said earlier

    Condition: if, unless

- *To preview the organization of your presentation*

  "First, briefly, I'd like to review the causes of _____.
    Then I will offer three possible solutions to this problem."
  "I will first describe the parts of the machine, and then I can
    explain how they work."
  "Let me first explain what we've done on the project so far,
    and then I can tell you what our future plans are."

- *To start with the first main point*

  "The first advantage (reason, step) is _____."
  "Let's start first with the major cause of the problem."

- *To add other main points*

  "The second (third, fourth) main effect is _____."
  "That, then, is the first advantage of _____. Let's
    take a look at another important advantage."
  "Let's move on to another main _____."

- *To move from one part of the presentation to another*

  "I now want to go on to _____."
  "Now that we've considered _____, let's turn to
    _____."
  "What are the advantages (disadvantages, results) of this
    plan?"

- *To end the presentation*

  "In conclusion (closing, summary), _____."
  "To conclude (summarize, sum up), _____."

ACTIVITY 7-D

1. Work individually to develop a three- to five-minute presentation
   on a topic of your choice. In planning your presentation, concentrate on using transitions effectively to move from point to point,
   to fit ideas together, and to connect different parts of your
   presentation.
2. Now work in groups. Take turns giving your presentations to the
   group. Take notes on the points presented by the speaker along
   with the transitions used to connect these ideas. After each
   speaker has finished, discuss the strengths and weaknesses of the
   transitions. How smoothly did the speaker move from point to

point? How effectively were the different ideas and parts of the presentation connected?

3. After everyone has practiced in groups, some of you may be asked to give your presentations to the entire class.

Presentation Assignment 3

After studying the information in this unit, you can prepare a five- to six-minute presentation to give to a group or to the entire class. Look at the presentation evaluation form on page 114 to see how you will be evaluated. You can use the following guidelines to help you prepare your presentation:

1. Your instructor may assign a topic or allow you to choose your own. A list of suggested presentation assignments follows this list of guidelines, but you should choose a specific topic based on your knowledge and experience. If possible, your topic should relate to your major or field of specialization. You may want to refer again to Worksheet 1 on page 241 of Appendix I to help you think of a topic.
2. Analyze your audience. You may want to look over Worksheet 2 on page 246 of Appendix I. If you haven't yet filled that out, you can do so now.
3. Review the ideas you brainstormed earlier. After considering the characteristics of your listeners, try to select several topics that would be suitable for class presentations. Ask yourself these questions about each topic:
   A. Do you know enough about this topic?
   B. If some research is needed, do you have the time and resources to find the information?
   C. Have you limited the topic enough so that you can cover it adequately in the time available?
   D. Is the topic of potential interest to your listeners?
   E. Is the topic too difficult or too technical for this audience?
   F. Is the topic too easy or too well-known to the audience?
4. Fill out a copy of Worksheet 3 on page 249 of Appendix I to turn in to your instructor. Consider any suggestions from your instructor before you make the final selection of the topic for your presentation.
5. Once you have determined the central idea of your presentation, decide which pattern of organization will best suit your topic.

Your instructor may ask you to turn in a copy of Worksheet 4 on page 250 of Appendix I.

6. Make notes of the information you want to include in your presentation. If you wish, do some additional research on your topic.

7. Make an outline of the points you want to present. Do not write out every word of your presentation. Check the outline to make sure that you have arranged the points in a logical order.

8. Plan your introduction and conclusion.

9. Review your outline until you know the material very well. Do not, however, try to memorize all of the information.

10. You can write brief notes on small note cards to help you remember the order of the main points that you want to present.

11. If you wish, prepare a short list of any specialized or technical terms or concepts that you are going to use in your presentation. Make sure that you know how to explain these to your listeners in clear, simple English.

12. Before giving your presentation, check with the instructor or a dictionary about the correct pronunciation of any new or unfamiliar vocabulary words.

13. Using your notes, practice giving your presentation several times before you have to give it in class. During practice make sure that your presentation meets the time requirements of the assignment.

Suggested Topics

1. Give an analysis of something.

   Sample topics:
      uses of lasers in medicine
      sources of radiation in the environment
      applications of fiber-optic technology
      ways to dispose of toxic wastes
      uses of synthetic polymers
      advantages of organically grown food
      uses of radioisotopes
      dangers of radon in the environment
      effects of biotechnology on agriculture
      ways to improve the university curriculum in a particular
         field of study

2. Give a physical description of something.

Sample topics:
    a DNA molecule
    a lighthouse
    the brain
    a cable bridge (a suspension bridge)
    a dinosaur
    Mars (Mercury, Venus, Jupiter, etc.)
    a comet
    a pneumatic gripper
    a bat
    an electric motor

Guidelines:

A. A physical description includes the answers to the following questions:
  • What is it?
  • What does it do?/What is it used for?
  • What does it look like? (size, weight, shape, color, composition)
  • What are the main parts that make up the whole?
  • How do these parts fit together?
  • What is the function or purpose of each part?

B. Since this is a physical description, emphasize the physical characteristics rather than its operation.

C. Do not include so many details that the listeners are confused.

3. Describe a simple mechanism or object without identifying it. As you describe the object, the rest of the students in the class should be trying to draw a picture of it. At the end of your presentation, show the students your drawing of the object.

4. Give a functional description of a mechanism or an object.

Sample topics:
    a microwave oven
    an air conditioning unit
    the respiratory (digestive, circulatory) system
    a beehive
    a weather satellite
    a canal lock
    a hydrofoil
    self-developing film
    a coral colony
    the pituitary (thyroid, adrenal, thymus) gland

Guidelines:

A. A functional description explains how something works. It is different from a description of a process in that it emphasizes the working of one thing or object rather than the steps people need to take in order to complete an operation.

B. The presentation should include:
- a general description
- a division of the device into components (what each part is, its purpose, its appearance)
- an explanation of the sequences of the operation
- an explanation of the scientific principles by which it operates

C. A visual aid, such as the actual object, a photograph, a drawing, or a diagram will help clarify your description.

5. Discuss a problem, emphasizing the causes.

Sample problems:

the possible use of biological weapons
the depletion of the earth's ozone layer
smog
computer crime
saving a specific endangered species (eagles, dolphins, whales)
urban slums
acquiring organs for transplants
deforestation in a particular country
scientific fraud
infant mortality in a particular region

Guidelines:

The presentation should include:
- a description of the problem
- an explanation of the significance of the problem
- any necessary background of the problem
- causes of the problem
- solutions to the problem

6. Discuss a problem, emphasizing possible solutions.
Sample problems: See sample problems listed in #5.

7. Discuss a problem, recommending the best solution(s).
Sample problems: See sample problems listed in #5.

Guidelines:

The presentation should include:
- a description of the problem
- an explanation of the recommended solution
- reasons that this is the best solution to the problem

Suggested Assignments for Listeners

The instructor may assign different students to do some of the following listening assignments. The listeners should then turn in their assignments to the instructor, give them to the speaker, or discuss their results with the rest of the group or class, according to the teacher's instructions.

1. Fill out the evaluation form.
2. Write two questions to ask the speaker about the presentation.
3. Pay particular attention to the organization of the report. Consider the following questions in analyzing the organization:
   A. What was the central idea of the presentation?
   B. What pattern of organization did the speaker follow?
   C. What were the main points presented by the speaker?
   D. Were the main points presented in a logical way?
4. Pay particular attention to the way the speaker used transitions. What transitions did the speaker use to move from one point to another?

Presentation Evaluation 3

Speaker: _____

Topic: _____

Evaluator: _____

Rating System
Complete the following evaluation form by filling in the appropriate number of points in the blanks provided. The point values are as follows:

2 = Excellent   1 = Satisfactory   0 = Needs Improvement

These points can be added up to give a total score for each section on the form. Follow your teacher's instructions in rating the speaker on one, two, or all of the sections included in this form. Space is provided on the form for your comments on specific strengths or weaknesses of the speaker's presentation. You can also add suggestions for improving future presentations.

I. *Delivery*

Points out of 10: _____   *Comments:*

_____ A. volume—loud enough to be heard clearly
_____ B. eye contact with audience
_____ C. natural delivery—not read or memorized
_____ D. rate of speech—not too fast or too slow
_____ E. posture/body movement—no distracting mannerisms

II. *Content*

Points out of 10: _____   *Comments:*

_____ A. clear central idea
_____ B. topic suitable for time available—not too limited or too general

_____ C. topic suitable for this
audience—not too techni-
cal or too well-known

_____ D. topic developed with
relevant details, facts,
examples that provide
strong support of central
idea

_____ E. presentation meets time
requirements—not too
long or too short

III. *Organization*

Points out of 10: _____   *Comments:*

_____ A. introduction

_____ B. use of transitions

_____ C. main points clearly stated

_____ D. development of ideas
logical, easy to follow

_____ E. conclusion

Total Number of Points Received by Speaker: _____

Total Number of Possible Points: _____

Questions to ask the speaker:

1. _____

2. _____

Clarifying to make clear

Expressions

The following list includes only some of the many possible expressions that are used to convey each function. Space is provided for you to add other expressions related to each function as you work through the unit. Before going over the lists provided, you may want to discuss each function and then work individually or in small groups to list expressions that you are already familiar with. You can then identify any expressions that seem to be particularly formal, informal, direct, or indirect and then compare them with those listed here. You might also discuss possible situations in which these expressions could appropriately be used.

> *Asking for clarification*
> What do you mean?
> What does _____ʊ_____ mean?
> What do you mean by ___that___?
> Do you mean _____?
> I'm sorry, but I didn't follow you. Could you please
>
> $\begin{Bmatrix} \text{repeat} \\ \text{explain} \end{Bmatrix}$ what you said?
>
> I'm not sure what you mean.
>
> Sorry, but I don't $\begin{Bmatrix} \text{understand} \\ \text{see} \end{Bmatrix}$ what you mean.

Clarifying
   I mean _____.
   In other words, _____.
   What I mean is that _____.
   The point I'm trying to make is _____.

Paraphrasing (try to make it clear)
   I think he [or she] means _____.
   What he [or she] means is that _____.
   In other words, he [or she] means _____.
   I think his [or her] point is that _____.

Asking for further information
   Would you mind explaining that a little more, please?
   Could you tell us more about that?
   Could you please explain that in a little more detail?
   Could you be more specific?

Listening Practice

The following exercises can be completed by listening to Unit 8 on the tape.

Section 1.   There are eight short dialogs in this section. Each one is about a different subject.

A.   Before you listen to the dialogs, look at the list of words below. How many do you know? Work individually or with a partner to write brief definitions of the words that you know.

Vocabulary	Definitions
1. to demolish	to destroy, clean the plan
2. to implement	to use, work more details
3. cost-effective	it works some money
4. feasible	practical, more carefully
5. to sue	take to court.
6. controversial	not opposit
7. affordable	able to handle
8. to exploit	to take advantage

B. Now listen to Section 1 on the tape. Put a check [✓] next to the definitions that are correct. Write or revise the definition of each word as you understand its meaning from the dialog.

C. Work with a partner, in a small group, or as a class to compare your definitions.

Section 2. There are six short dialogs in this section. Each one is about a different subject.

A. Listen to Section 2 on the tape. Write the expression each speaker uses to ask for clarification or further information.

Expressions

1. _I don't understand what_
2. _let me see what I follow you_
3. _Could you explain that in a little more detail_
4. _Could you be more specific_
5. _Could you explain what they are_
6. _____

B. Listen again. Work individually to write brief answers to the following questions:

1. What is oral rehydration therapy?

using the solution such as to water mixing with salt and sugar

2. How has the leisure industry been revolutionized?

The technology change the leisure time by invented new product such as Car, TV, et.

3. What is "blue skies" research?

inventing a new commercial and potential

4. Why would using a growth hormone to increase milk production be disastrous to the dairy industry?

because we need less milk in the Market then we have kill more cows

5. What are CFCs?

Sources of cloris carbon of chemical.

6. Why does the man refer to the infant mortality rate as a "disgrace"?

because we didn't pay enough care to infant before birth

C. Work with a partner, in a small group, or as a class to compare your answers in Parts A and B.

Controlled Practice

Exercise 1. Use some different expressions from the unit in discussing the photographs on page 121.

Speaker A: Make a statement or give your opinion.

Speaker B: Ask for clarification or further information about what the speaker said.

Speaker A: Clarify the point or give further information.

Exercise 2. Before doing this exercise in class, you may have to do some preparation. Find out what each of the following words, phenomena, scientific principles, or laws means. Then be able to explain it in your own words.

Student A: Make a sentence such as "An article I'm reading deals with _____."

Student B: Ask for clarification or further information.

Student A: Clarify the point or give further information.

General Interest

1. meteors — *small piece of matter floating in space*
2. local area networks (LANS)
3. telecommunications satellites
4. jet streams — *white line on sky*
5. android robots — *human robot*

Science

6. hydroponics — *science growing plant*
7. the "green revolution" *change in the farming*
8. sunspots —
9. photosynthesis
10. Brownian motion —

Engineering

11. desalination — *take away the salt*
12. reinforced concrete
13. thermodynamics —
14. Ohm's law — *unit to measure electricity*
15. transistors —

Health

16. histology — *study about body cells*
17. immunity — *fight against the disease*
18. pulmonary circulation — *Lungs*
19. placebos — *fake, not real → imagination*
20. the endocrine system —

Exercise 3. Complete the following sentences. Be prepared to explain your ideas. Use a variety of expressions from the unit.

Student A: Complete the sentence with an opinion.

Student B: Ask for clarification or further information.

Student A: Clarify the statement or give further information.

General Interest

1. Deforestation _____.
2. The problem of acid rain _____.
3. Wind energy _____.
4. Mining metals on the bottom of the ocean _____.
5. Cordless telephones _____.
6. Nuclear energy _____.
7. Saving whales _____.
8. Space exploration _____.
9. It's difficult for many researchers to _____.
10. Controlling population growth _____.

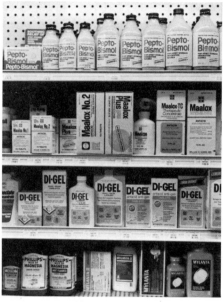

1. over-the-counter medicine

2. traditional crafts

3. community health programs

4. electron microscopes

Science

11. Cloning _____.
12. Radioactive waste _____.
13. Asbestos _____.
14. Scientists have a responsibility to _____.
15. Noise pollution _____.

Engineering

16. Lasers _____.
17. Cloverleaf interchanges _____.
18. Improving sanitation _____.
19. High-speed trains _____.
20. Supersonic jets _____.

Health

21. Aspirin _____.
22. Surgery _____.
23. Ultrasound _____.
24. Amphetamines _____.
25. Powdered baby formula _____.

Communication Concepts

STEPS IN PROBLEM SOLVING

Discussion groups are most efficient when they follow a logical step-by-step procedure in problem solving. The most common procedure that effective groups use is the problem-solution pattern of problem solving. Following this pattern, the group first analyzes the problem and then moves on to the solution stage of the discussion. If all group members are familiar with this pattern, the discussion will move in a much more organized manner. The problem-solution pattern includes the steps discussed here.

1. *Defining and analyzing the problem*

   The group needs to develop a clear statement of the problem to be solved. Once the problem is defined, the group can begin to analyze it. The purpose of this step is to bring out different viewpoints and facts so that everyone has a clear understanding of all the factors involved in the problem. The following questions should be considered:

- What are the facts of the situation?
- How serious or harmful is the problem?
- What is the history or background of the problem?
- What are the causes of the problem?
- What are the effects of the problem?

2. *Determining criteria to judge solutions*

The next step is for the group to establish the standards, or criteria, that the ideal solution should meet. Criteria are important because they give the group a basis for judging the strengths and weaknesses of possible solutions. Group members may agree, for example, that the solution they want must meet the following criteria:

- The solution must not cost more than X amount of money.
- The solution must not take more than X amount of time to put into effect.
- The solution must be practical.
- The solution must be acceptable to everyone in the discussion group.

3. *Suggesting solutions*

Next, members brainstorm ideas to develop a list of all possible solutions to the problem. During this brainstorming session members try to think of as many solutions as possible without stopping to judge the quality of the ideas. Then, after a list has been drawn up, the group can choose three or four solutions to discuss in more detail.

4. *Evaluating solutions*

Now the group is ready to discuss and evaluate the proposed solutions, one by one. After a solution has been explained, group members should work together to bring out its advantages and disadvantages. The group evaluates each solution by checking to see how well it meets the criteria developed earlier. This is not the time for participants to bring up other solutions to compare with the one under discussion. If other solutions are brought up at this point, the discussion can lose its direction and become quite disorganized. After the group has thoroughly analyzed one solution, the leader can bring up the next one for discussion. Of course, members should consider all of the proposed solutions before trying to make a final decision.

5. *Selecting the best solution*

After all the suggestions have been discussed, the group members need to compare the different solutions in terms of how well they meet the established criteria. Clearly, the group should choose the solution or combination of solutions that has the most advantages and the fewest disadvantages. The group should try to reach a consensus on the best solution to the problem.

Discussion Techniques

GETTING A POINT INTO THE DISCUSSION

At times you may find it difficult to work your way into a discussion. You may find it helpful to gain the attention of the other group members by introducing what you are going to say with a comment or question. This technique is especially useful in a discussion since it makes the listeners aware of your intentions and leads to clearer communication.

I have a $\left\{ \begin{array}{l} \text{suggestion} \\ \text{point} \end{array} \right\}$ I'd like to make.

I have a question I'd like to ask.

May I $\left\{ \begin{array}{l} \text{ask a question?} \\ \text{add something here?} \\ \text{make a suggestion?} \end{array} \right.$

Discussion Practice

RANKING IN ORDER

The cases in this section are designed to give you practice in ranking items in order of their importance. Since this type of decision is a matter of opinion rather than fact, there is no right or wrong order. The purpose of these discussion role plays is to give you practice in working as a group to reach a final decision by consensus.

Instructions

1. Get into small groups. All groups may be assigned to work on the same case in order to compare results, or groups may work on different cases according to their particular interests.

2. Work individually to rank the five most important items (criteria, aspects, features, or activities) from 1 to 5. Put number 1 for the most important, number 2 for the next most important, and so forth to number 5. Do not discuss your choices with the other members of your group.
3. Now work in your group. Choose a group leader. Compare and discuss your ideas. Then work together to agree on a common listing. As a group, rank the items in order from 1 to 5. Prepare to present and defend your choices to other groups.
4. If other groups have worked on the same case, compare rankings. Explain the reasons for your final choices.
5. When you have finished, complete the Participant Evaluation Form on page 130.

CASE 1: SELECTING SPEAKING ACTIVITIES

Situation

An American multinational company employs many professionals in the fields of science and engineering who do not speak English as their native language. Company officials have asked the training department to organize a course in oral communication skills in English for these professionals. The training department has asked a group of these employees to draw up a list of the kinds of speaking situations in which they need the most practice. The training department can then develop a course relevant to the needs of these employees.

The most useful speaking skills to include in the course are:

_____ 1. formal speeches to large audiences

_____ 2. oral presentations with visual aids

_____ 3. telephone conversation skills

_____ 4. group discussions with nontechnical personnel

_____ 5. one-to-one talks with experts

_____ 6. social/conversation skills

_____ 7. one-to-one talks with nontechnical personnel

_____ 8. group discussions with technical personnel

_____ 9. informal presentations to a few people

_____ 10. job interview skills

_____ **11.** _____

_____ **12.** _____

CASE 2: ATTRACTING OUTSTANDING SCIENTISTS

Situation

Executives of a company are interested in attracting outstanding scientists to join their growing organization. In order to decide how to attract these people, they would like to determine which aspects of work scientists consider to be most important. They have asked members of the scientific community to indicate the most important aspects of job satisfaction.

The most important aspects of job satisfaction are:

_____ **1.** a high salary with good fringe benefits

_____ **2.** a cooperative, friendly work atmosphere

_____ **3.** flexible working hours

_____ **4.** having the freedom to manage your own work and initiate new projects

_____ **5.** working with others who are outstanding in their field

_____ **6.** promotion opportunities

_____ **7.** working for an organization with a good reputation

_____ **8.** the opportunity to participate in policy and business decisions

_____ **9.** a competitive, challenging work atmosphere

_____ **10.** job security

_____ **11.** _____

_____ **12.** _____

CASE 3: CHOOSING USEFUL COURSES

Situation

Science professionals have complained that their university education did not provide them with enough knowledge of subjects outside their area of specialization. A local university is conducting a survey to determine which of the following courses would be most beneficial to students as future science professionals. The university has asked science professionals to recommend certain courses to include as requirements in addition to the usual core courses of a student's specialization.

The most useful courses are:

_____   **1.**   calculus

_____   **2.**   statistics

_____   **3.**   creative problem solving

_____   **4.**   speed reading

_____   **5.**   data processing

_____   **6.**   oral communication skills

_____   **7.**   survey of computer applications

_____   **8.**   logic

_____   **9.**   business management

_____   **10.**   economics

_____   **11.**   psychology

_____   **12.**   world history

_____   **13.**   technical writing

_____   **14.**   _____

_____   **15.**   _____

CASE 4: DESIGNING A PUBLIC PARK

Situation

A city has received funds to develop a small area of land on the edge of town into a public park. Because members of the city council will soon be asking for bids on the project, they need to draw up a list of the features that they consider to be essential in a good public park. Unfortunately, the amount of money is limited, so not all possible features can be included in the park.

The most important features to include in every park design are:

_____ 1. a swimming pool

_____ 2. grassy areas

_____ 3. jogging/bicycle paths

_____ 4. flower gardens

_____ 5. food stands

_____ 6. barbecue facilities

_____ 7. picnic tables

_____ 8. sports facilities for football, volleyball, etc.

_____ 9. many trees

_____ 10. bandstand area for concerts, plays, etc.

_____ 11. an artificial lake

_____ 12. playground facilities for children

_____ 13. _____

_____ 14. _____

CASE 5: AWARDING A GRANT

Situation

A nonprofit organization has announced plans to provide scholar-ships and financial awards to promising high school students. The purpose of these grants is to encourage national scientific advancement by discovering and developing scientific ability among high school students. This organization has asked a group of scientists to help establish the criteria for choosing the students who should receive the scholarships or awards.

The organization should choose students who:

_____ 1. have high overall grades in all school subjects

_____ 2. participate extensively in extracurricular activities

_____ 3. show financial need

_____ 4. are regarded as good creative thinkers by teachers

_____ 5. have excellent grades in science and math courses

_3_ **6.** score high on a national science achievement test

_____ **7.** are involved in community service projects

_3_ **8.** write the best essay on the topic of "My Future Professional Goals"

_2_ **9.** receive excellent recommendations from teachers

_4_ **10.** have demonstrated scientific ability by completing research projects or winning awards

_____ **11.** _____

_____ **12.** _____

CASE 6: APPLYING SCIENCE TO A SOCIAL PROBLEM

Situation

The National Science Foundation is planning to sponsor a project to show how state-of-the-art advances in science and technology can be used to benefit society as a whole. The foundation wants to develop innovative applications of science to one particular area not directly related to the field of science. A panel of scientists has been asked to recommend a social problem to be the focus of the project.

  The panel should choose the social problem of:

_____ **1.** mental health

_____ **2.** poverty

_____ **3.** world hunger

_____ **4.** urbanization

_____ **5.** unemployment

_____ **6.** overpopulation

_____ **7.** crime

_____ **8.** discrimination

_____ **9.** illiteracy

_____ **10.** old age

_____ **11.** _____

_____ **12.** _____

Discussion Evaluation

PARTICIPANT EVALUATION FORM

1. Identifying the group
   A. Discussion topic: _____
   B. Names of other students in your group: _____
   _____

2. Did all group members take an active part in reaching the final decision?
   _____

3. Did you change your mind about the order of ranking during the discussion? Why or why not?
   _____
   _____

4. Did any particular group member(s) influence your decision? How or why did they have this effect?
   _____
   _____

5. How long did it take to reach a final decision?
   _____

6. How was the leader chosen?
   _____ A. general agreement
   _____ B. voting
   _____ C. someone volunteered
   _____ D. the instructor appointed someone
   _____ E. _____

7. Do you think that this was the best way to choose a leader? Why or why not?
   _____
   _____
   _____

8. How did the group reach a decision?
   _____ A. *Consensus.* The group reached a general agreement.
   _____ B. *Majority rule.* The group chose the item(s) that more than half of the members agreed on.

_____ C. *Voting.* Since there was no clear majority for an item, the members voted and those items with the most votes won.

_____ D. *Authority.* The leader or a strong participant pushed through a decision.

_____ E. *Default.* The group could not reach a decision.

_____ F. *Other.* _____

9. How do you think your group could have improved the decision-making process?

_____

_____

_____

Analyzing Solutions 1

Expressions

Solutions (suggestions, proposals, plans, actions, rules, regulations, or laws) may be analyzed according to a number of different criteria. This unit focuses on only three possible criteria: cost, time, and side effects. In a discussion, group members ask questions, support, and/ or oppose possible solutions with these and other criteria in mind. Before going over the expressions provided, you may want to discuss each function and then work individually or in small groups to list expressions that you are already familiar with. You can compare them with the ones listed here and then put a plus sign (+) next to those expressions that support and a minus sign (−) next to those that oppose a solution. As usual, the expressions listed are only some of the many possible ways of conveying each idea, so you may want to add other expressions or points to those included here.

Asking about cost
Is the solution economical?
Is the cost reasonable?
Do we have enough money to pay for this?

What will this solution cost to $\begin{cases} \text{implement?} \\ \text{maintain?} \end{cases}$

Analyzing cost

The solution $\left\{ \begin{array}{l} \text{is} \\ \text{isn't} \end{array} \right\}$ very economical.

The cost is $\left\{ \begin{array}{l} \text{reasonable.} \\ \text{unreasonable.} \end{array} \right.$

It's worth the cost.

It isn't worth the money.

It $\left\{ \begin{array}{l} \text{won't} \\ \text{will} \end{array} \right\}$ cost too much [money].

We have plenty of money to cover the costs.

We don't have enough money to cover the costs.

It's cost-effective.

It's a waste of money.

Asking about time

How long will it take to get results?

Will this solution have an immediate effect?

Is this a permanent or only a temporary solution?

Will it have a long-term effect?

Analyzing time

This solution will have an immediate effect.

This solution will take too long to get results.

It's $\left\{ \begin{array}{l} \text{worth the} \\ \text{a waste of} \end{array} \right\}$ time.

It's a long-term solution.

It's only a short-term solution.

$\left. \begin{array}{l} \text{It's} \\ \text{It isn't} \end{array} \right\}$ worth the time it will take to get results.

Asking about side effects

Will the solution create new problems?

Will this plan require $\left\{ \begin{array}{l} \text{a lot of paperwork?} \\ \text{a lot of meetings?} \\ \text{firing any employees?} \\ \text{retraining current workers?} \end{array} \right.$

Analyzing side effects

The solution { will not create any new problems.
may cause even worse problems, such as

_____.

The advantages { outweigh
don't outweigh } the disadvantages.

The drawbacks are minimal compared to the possible
benefits.

The solution could have some negative side effects.
For example, _____.

Listening Practice

The following exercises can be completed by listening to Unit 9 on the
tape.

Section 1.   There are eight separate dialogs in this section. They are
all based on the same general subject: automating an office.

A.   Listen to Section 1 on the tape. Check [✓] the criterion mentioned in each dialog.

	Cost	Time	Side Effects		Cost	Time	Side Effects
1.	___	✓	✓	5.	___	✓	___
2.	___	___	✓	6.	___	✓	✓
3.	✓	✓	✓	7.	___	✓	___
4.	___	___	✓	8.	___	___	✓

B.   Work with a partner, in a small group, or as a class to compare
your answers.

Section 2.   There are five separate dialogs in this section. They are all
based on the same general subject. Members of the Water Resources
Control Board are discussing what action should be taken to clean up
polluted water in a wildlife sanctuary. The water is polluted because
local farmers dump the water drained from their irrigated fields into
the park. Over the years toxic materials have accumulated in the water, thus causing the present problem.

A.   Listen to Section 2 on the tape. Check [✔] the criterion used to analyze each suggestion offered in this discussion.

Solutions	Criteria		
	Cost	Time	Side Effects
1. stop all farming in the area			✔
2. channel the water into the ocean			✔
3. forbid the use of toxins			✔
4. build a water treatment plant	✔		✔
5. put the water treatment plant into operation		✔	

B.   Listen again. Decide whether the second speaker supports or opposes the solution. Put a check [✔] in the correct space and then write the expression the speaker uses.

	Support	Oppose	Expressions
1.			
2.			
3.			
4.			
5.			

C.   Work with a partner, in a small group, or as a class to compare your answers.

Controlled Practice

Exercise 1.   Use some different expressions from the unit in discussing the illustrations on page 137.

Exercise 2.   Each of the following is a technical problem with many possible solutions. One solution for each problem is offered in the exercise. This solution may have many advantages or it may have many disadvantages, according to the criteria in the unit. Analyze each solution to determine its strengths and weaknesses by using appropriate expressions from the unit.

Student A: Explain the problem and give the solution.

Student B: Ask a question about the solution.

Student A: Answer the question with any reasonable response.

Student C: Ask another question.

Student A: Answer the question.

General Interest

1. *Problem:* Only about 800 wild giant pandas still exist, mainly in one country.

   Solution: The local government should put all these pandas in zoos.

2. *Problem:* The government is concerned over possible security problems caused by allowing foreign students to have access to supercomputers.

   Solution: The government should ban foreign students from enrolling in courses that use supercomputers.

3. *Problem:* A country wants to use technology to help develop rural communities.

   Solution: The government can provide villages with televisions and broadcast regular programs dealing with village improvement.

Science

4. *Problem:* Killer bees have escaped from a research laboratory.

   Solution: The laboratory should spray the area with a pesticide to kill the bees.

5. *Problem:* Four rare white tiger cubs have been born in captivity. The mother refuses to nurse them. One has already died.

   Solution: Zoo officials should take the cubs away from the mother and nurse them in the laboratory.

6. *Problem:* Many houses in a community are infested with mice.

   Solution: The government should supply free mouse traps to the residents.

Engineering

7. *Problem:* A poorly designed nuclear reactor has exploded.

   Solution: Officials can close off the area to prevent the spread of pollutants.

Solutions?

What About Cost?   Time?   Side Effects?

1. nuclear energy to generate electricity

2. free nutrition classes to fight malnutrition

3. an anti-litter campaign to clean up dirty cities

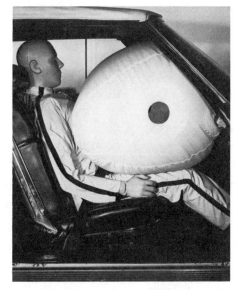

4. air bags to reduce traffic fatalities

8. *Problem:* Slum buildings in a major city are crowded and in poor condition.

   Solution: The government can knock down the buildings and build new housing for the people in these areas.

9. *Problem:* Traditional industry in areas such as textiles, leather work, and carpet making are dying as traditional workers move to the modern sector.

   Solution: Engineers can help provide technology to improve the quality of traditional crafts.

Health

10. *Problem:* A measles epidemic is spreading through a community.

    Solution: Health officials should immunize everyone in the community.

11. *Problem:* Government clinics supply free medicine to patients. Many patients take the medicine home, but they do not use it.

    Solution: The patients should pay for their medicine.

12. *Problem:* Leukemia appears seven times more often among people who have spent their lives with smokers.

    Solution: Doctors should advise nonsmokers to avoid all contact with smokers.

Exercise 3. Go back to the previous exercise. This time think of your own solution to each problem.

   Student A: Explain the problem and suggest your own solution.

   Student B: Ask a question about the solution.

   Student A: Answer the question with any reasonable response.

   Student C: Ask another question.

   Student A: Answer the question.

Communication Concepts

EFFECTIVE LISTENING

One advantage of making decisions in a small group is that the different group members bring a variety of facts and opinions to contribute to the discussion. This advantage will be lost completely if the participants do not listen to and understand all of the ideas expressed by the other group members. Thus, it is easy to see why effective listening is an essential skill in small group communication. By being a good listener, you encourage others to explain and develop their ideas. Furthermore, the best way to get others to listen carefully to your ideas is for you to listen to theirs.

One difficulty with listening comprehension is that many people have poor listening habits. For example, some people are more interested in talking than in listening. Others think about what they are going to say next rather than listening to what the speaker is saying. Another problem is that some people only listen to what interests them or what they already believe and do not bother to pay attention to anything else. In any case, good listening is a skill that can be improved by following these guidelines:

1. Give the speaker all of your attention. Do not take unnecessary notes, look through papers, or draw pictures while the speaker is talking.
2. Be patient. Let the speaker finish before you begin to speak. If you interrupt, the speaker may feel that you are not interested in what he or she has to say.
3. If you disagree with what the other person is saying, try to get a full understanding of that point of view before you speak. You may want to repeat or paraphrase the other person's idea to make sure that you have understood it correctly.
4. If another person is making a point that you disagree with, do *not* plan what you are going to say while that speaker is still talking. If you are trying to think of what to say next, you cannot pay attention to the speaker's entire message.
5. Ask for clarification if you do not understand what the speaker has said. Also, ask questions to encourage the speaker and to show that you are listening.
6. Listen for the main ideas that the speaker is communicating. Examine the facts or examples that the speaker uses to support the main ideas. Ask yourself whether these points are relevant and reasonable.
7. Try to judge what the speaker says rather than how well he or she says it. It is the content of the message that is important, not the delivery.
8. Use suitable body language to encourage other speakers: look directly at people when they are speaking, smile sometimes, and nod when you agree with what they have said.

Discussion Techniques

AVOIDING ANSWERING

There are times in a discussion when someone asks you a question that you are unable to answer. It may be that you don't have the necessary information or that you have not thought enough about a point to offer an opinion. It is also possible that you are explaining an idea or suggestion that is still in the planning stage, so you haven't worked out all of the details yet. In any case, if you simply remain silent when someone asks you a question, the discussion can slow down or stop while everybody is waiting for an answer. The discussion may also lose direction if group members start trying to explain the question to you, thinking that you didn't understand it. Therefore, you need to make it clear right away that you don't have an answer:

I'm afraid I $\left\{ \begin{array}{l} \text{don't know.} \\ \text{can't answer your question.} \end{array} \right.$

Frankly, I don't really know.

I can't really say.

It's $\left\{ \begin{array}{l} \text{difficult} \\ \text{impossible} \end{array} \right\}$ to say.

After saying that you can't answer, you can keep the discussion moving and try to satisfy the questioner by adding an appropriate remark such as:

Perhaps someone else can answer that.

All of the details haven't been worked out yet, but I'll let you know when I have something more definite.

I'll check with _____ and get back to you with that information.

Discussion Practice

SOLVING A PROBLEM

The cases in this section will give you further practice in participating in problem-solving discussions.

Instructions

1. Refer to the detailed instructions included in the Discussion Practice section of Unit 2 for guidance in choosing cases, getting organized, brainstorming, selecting ideas, preparing for, and starting the discussion.
2. After participating in the discussion, all group members can complete the Participant Self-Evaluation Form on page 145. Group observers should complete the Observer Evaluation Form on page 147 as directed by the instructor. They can then discuss their evaluations with the group members. If other groups have worked on the same case, compare your solutions.

CASE 1: BRAIN DRAIN

Situation

A recent UNESCO (United Nations Educational, Scientific and Cultural Organization) study has focused on the severe shortage of technically trained personnel in some developing countries. Specifically, twelve countries have only thirty to sixty scientists per million people. These statistics show the developing countries' immediate need for highly trained scientists and technicians.

   The problem is that in these countries few people are trained in science and technology. Moreover, those few people who are trained often leave their native countries after a few years or never return from their studies overseas. Many of these people say that this is due to the unsatisfactory research situation at home. A number of developing countries have joined with UNESCO to find a solution to this lack of scientific and technological experts. A meeting has been called to discuss the problem.

Purpose of the Discussion

Group members should try to agree on the best way to increase the number of local scientists and technicians in developing countries.

Group Roles

The following people take part in the discussion:

> Leader: a representative from UNESCO
> Representative(s) from the government of a developing
>   country
> Scientist(s) from a developing country now living overseas

CASE 2: PANIC OVER FRUIT

Situation

An anonymous telephone call warned officials from the Food and Drug Department that fruit imported from a major fruit-producing country had been poisoned. After examining thousands of crates of fruit shipped from that country, officials discovered two grapes that had been injected with cyanide. Food and Drug Department officials are now considering destroying all the fruit imported from this country because there is no quick way to test for liquid-cyanide poisoning in fruit. This country, however, provides almost all of the grapes, peaches, blueberries, blackberries, melons, pears, and plums on the market this time of year. Furthermore, the government of the fruit-producing country is protesting that their $500 million fruit and vegetable industry will be ruined and more than 200,000 workers will lose their jobs if this action is taken. The State Department has called a meeting to discuss both sides of the issue.

Purpose of the Discussion

Group members should try to agree on the best action to take regarding the poisoned fruit.

Group Roles

The following people take part in the discussion:

> Leader: a State Department official
> Representative(s) from the Food and Drug Department
> Representative(s) from the fruit-producing country

CASE 3: STREETS FOR PEOPLE

Situation

The city center of one community has suffered a major drop in business as people have turned to suburban shopping centers. To revitalize the city center, urban planners want to close the streets to traffic and build a pedestrian shopping mall. They say that increasing pedestrian space will improve the quality of the downtown environment. They also think that a pedestrian mall will encourage new investment. The downtown area can be made competitive with suburban shopping centers. Traffic engineers are opposed to the plan. They believe that if streets are closed to create a pedestrian mall, traffic congestion on parallel streets will increase. Many business operators are also against the mall. They fear a further loss of business due to the drop in passing automobile traffic. City officials have called a meeting to discuss the issue.

Purpose of the Discussion

Group members should try to agree on the best way to revitalize the city center.

Group Roles

The following people take part in the discussion:

    Leader: a representative of the government
    Urban planner(s)
    Traffic engineer(s)
    Representative(s) of business

CASE 4: KIDNEY TRANSPLANTS

Situation

Hundreds of people in a community have died from kidney failure. The National Kidney Foundation (NKF) says that many lives can be saved if enough kidneys are available for transplantation. The foundation has asked for voluntary donations, but there has been little response. "Unfortunately," says a representative of the NKF, "few people will give one of their kidneys to a stranger." One patient has suggested paying people who donate a kidney. A staff member of the local hospital has suggested taking kidneys from dead people with or without their families' permission. A meeting has been called to discuss the situation.

Purpose of the Discussion

Group members should try to agree on the best way to acquire kidneys for transplantation.

Group Roles

The following people take part in the discussion:

> Leader: a representative of the National Kidney Foundation
> Representative(s) of patients in need of a kidney transplant
> Staff member(s) of the local hospital

Discussion Evaluation

A. PARTICIPANT SELF-EVALUATION FORM

After you participate in a group discussion, complete the following form:

1. *Rating your own performance.* Use the following scales to rate your own performance:

   A. *Interaction.* Did you effectively interact with others? Use a variety of functions? Initiate? Involve others? Ask questions?

Excellent	Satisfactory	Weak	Unsatisfactory
3	2	1	0

   B. *Use of Expressions.* Did you effectively and accurately use a variety of expressions?

Excellent	Satisfactory	Weak	Unsatisfactory
3	2	1	0

   C. *Content.* Did you contribute logical, relevant information and ideas? Stay on the subject? Analyze solutions? Show strong support of arguments?

Excellent	Satisfactory	Weak	Unsatisfactory
3	2	1	0

   D. *Accuracy.* Did you communicate ideas clearly with effective control of grammar, vocabulary, and pronunciation?

Excellent	Satisfactory	Weak	Unsatisfactory
3	2	1	0

2. *Improvement.* How do you think you have improved your speaking skills since the beginning of the course? Check any of the following that apply to you:

   _____ A. I feel more comfortable and self-confident when participating in a group discussion.

_____ B. I find it easier to speak in English now that I have had more practice in using the language.

_____ C. I am a more effective group participant than I was at the beginning of the course.

_____ D. I am a more effective discussion group leader than I was at the beginning of the course.

_____ E. My vocabulary has increased.

_____ F. My control of grammar has improved.

_____ G. My pronunciation has improved.

_____ H. I find it easier to understand other speakers.

_____ I. I find it easier to use expressions from the units.

_____ J. Other: _____

_____ K. Other: _____

3. *Action.* In what areas do you feel you still need to improve? What can you do on your own or in class to make these improvements? After filling in the following chart, work in pairs or small groups to compare ideas.

Areas to Improve	*Actions to Take*

B. OBSERVER EVALUATION FORM

1. *Listening to an individual.* In this discussion you should observe only one speaker.

    A. Speaker's name/role: _____

    B. Discussion topic: _____

2. *Listening for content and accuracy.* As you observe the discussion, pay close attention to the ideas that the speaker presents as well as the way in which these ideas are communicated. Look at the rating scales listed in #3. Use a separate sheet of paper to take notes in order to be able to rate the speaker according to these criteria.

3. *Rating the speaker.* Use the following scales to rate the speaker:

    A. *Content.* Did the speaker contribute logical, relevant information and ideas? Stay on the subject? Analyze solutions? Show strong support of arguments?

Excellent	Satisfactory	Weak	Unsatisfactory
3	2	1	0

    B. *Accuracy.* Did the speaker communicate ideas clearly with effective control of grammar, vocabulary, and pronunciation?

Excellent	Satisfactory	Weak	Unsatisfactory
3	2	1	0

4. *Making suggestions.* What suggestions can you make to help this speaker improve?

    _____

    _____

    _____

    _____

Providing Support

Presentation Preparation

DEVELOPING THE PRESENTATION

A. Finding Sources of Information

If someone asks you to give a presentation at work, you probably already know most of the information you must present. You may know the information as part of your job, or you may be presenting information that you have been gathering for a more formal written report. If research is necessary, you can usually obtain additional information from sources within your organization: from your company's library, from written reports, from data stored in a computer, or from other employees.

For a class presentation, you should choose a subject based on your own knowledge or experience. Of course, you may want to do some research to develop your topic in depth with accurate, up-to-date information. However, be sure that you have the time and ability to do any necessary research. If you need to do some research, the best place to begin looking for information on your subject is the library. If you are not sure how to use the library's resources, you can ask one of the staff for help. You might consider the following sources of printed information:

- almanacs
- annual reports
- atlases
- biographical registers

- books
- business handbooks
- dictionaries
- encyclopedias
- government documents
- newspapers
- pamphlets
- periodicals
- professional or trade journals

You can locate books on your subject by using the card catalog in the library. For a source of general information, you should become familiar with the *Readers' Guide to Periodical Literature,* which is an index of many popular magazines. In addition, there are other, more specialized indexes, such as the *Applied Science and Technology Index, Engineering Index, The Energy Index,* and *Index Medicus,* to help you locate current articles on your subject. The librarian can also help you locate articles by using a computerized data base, if available, to compile a list of sources on a particular subject. In addition to doing library research, you may also obtain information by interviewing experts in the field or through experimenting or observing. Furthermore, you can get information from radio and television broadcasts or from questionnaires and surveys.

ACTIVITY 10-A

1. If you would like to know more about research than is presented in this text, work individually or in small groups to prepare reports on some of the following topics:
   A. an explanation of the different types of cards found in the card catalog
   B. how to locate information on specific subjects using the card catalog
   C. an explanation of the book classification system used in your library, such as the Dewey Decimal System, the Library of Congress System, or the National Library of Medicine System
   D. how to locate books on the shelves of the library using the card catalog
   E. how to locate information on specific subjects using periodical indexes
   F. how to locate specific articles using periodical indexes
   G. a description of different kinds of reference materials found in the library
   H. how to use computer data banks to get information

ACTIVITY 10-B

1. Work individually or in small groups. Make a list of all periodical indexes and other reference books available in the library that relate to your major field.
2. If requested, you can make copies of your list to share with others in the class.

B. Gathering Information

Before starting to look for information on your topic, be sure to have a clear statement of your central idea. You then need to spend some time thinking about the subject in order to break it down into manageable units. It is important to find a natural grouping for your ideas in order to be able to present your information in a logical, understandable way. Using what you already know about the topic, decide what main ideas your presentation should probably cover. You should choose from two to five main headings under which you can organize all of the data you collect. Do not use more than five main ideas; five is the maximum number that people can easily follow and remember. Once you have decided on the probable main ideas of your presentation, you can put them in logical order to make a working outline of your presentation. This working outline of the main points will form the skeleton of your presentation. You can use it as a guide in collecting relevant facts, statistics, examples, and quotations to support each of the subtopics. As you gather information and learn more about the topic, you can change, add, or drop the headings so that a final plan of organization gradually takes shape.

As you collect data for your presentation, you should keep a record of all of the sources that you use. You can use one small note card to record each source, including the following information: name of the source (book or journal), title of the article, name of the author, publisher, copyright date, city where published, and pages used. You should code each one of these bibliography cards by writing a number on it. Then, when you photocopy or take notes from your sources, you can simply write down the number of the bibliography card plus the page number. Figure 10-A is an example of a bibliography card for a book. It is extremely important to keep track of your sources so that you will know where the information came from if you decide to use it in your presentation.

The best way to take notes is to use small index or note cards. You can put each idea or item on a note card and write the number of the bibliography card in the upper right hand corner of the card. Then, when you start organizing your presentation, you can easily arrange and rearrange these cards in the order that you want. Figure 10-B is an example of some notes taken from a resource book.

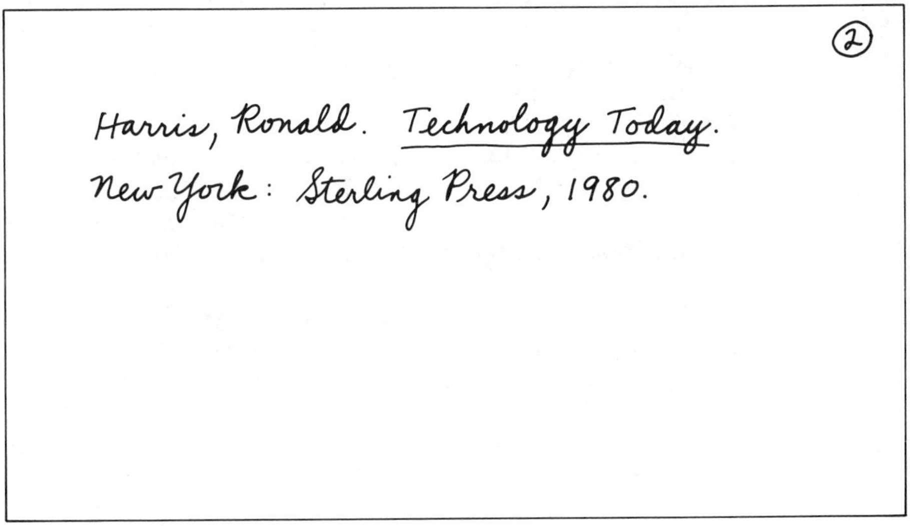

Harris, Ronald. *Technology Today.* New York: Sterling Press, 1980.

②

Figure 10-A

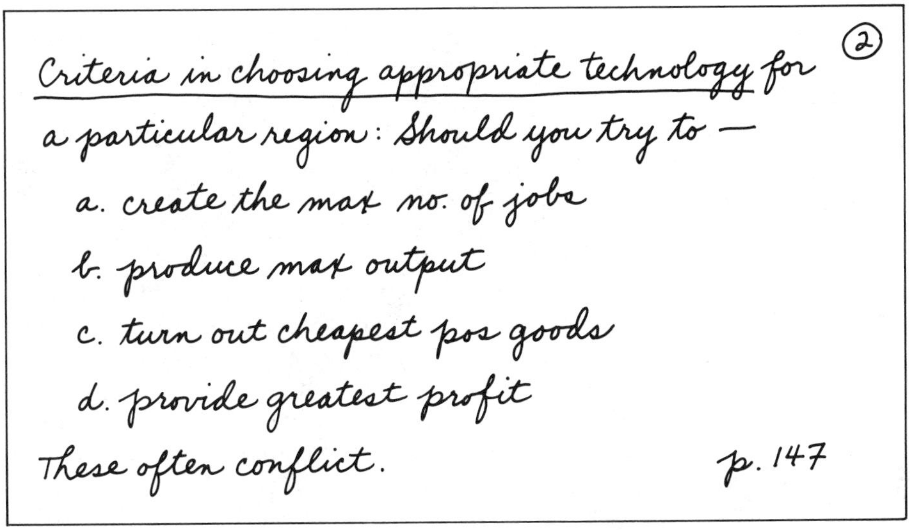

Criteria in choosing appropriate technology for a particular region: Should you try to —
a. create the max no. of jobs
b. produce max output
c. turn out cheapest pos goods
d. provide greatest profit
These often conflict.   p. 147

②

Figure 10-B

C. Arranging Your Material

Once you have collected the necessary material, you have to plan your presentation. The three basic parts of your presentation will be the introduction, the body, and the conclusion. First, you should work on the body of the presentation and then later you can develop the introduction and conclusion. The body is important because it contains the real content of your presentation—the development of your ideas. The body is where you present in detail the main points and subpoints of your presentation.

In order to organize all the information you have collected, you should start with the first main point on the final form of your working outline. Put all the note cards related to this point in a pile. Now you can decide what information to include and what to leave out of your final presentation. Put the note cards in some logical order. If you have not used note cards, then you can take a piece of paper and write down all the information that develops that particular point: details, facts, statistics, and examples. Once you have developed the first point, you can work on the others in the same way. Thus, you can begin to see the structure and development of your presentation.

D. Writing a Planning Outline

After you have sorted out your information in this way, you can begin writing the planning outline. Use your working outline and your note cards to write an outline that includes all of the information that you want to present. When you write your outline, be sure to use a format that lets you clearly separate the main ideas from the supporting details. For example, you might use Roman numbers [I, II, III, IV, V] for main points and capital letters [A, B, C, D, E] for subpoints. Then you can arrange the points in a logical order according to the pattern of organization you have chosen. By preparing this outline, you can see if your presentation is developed in a logical way with enough information to fully explore the topic.

While you are working on the planning outline, you can still make changes in your presentation; you can rearrange your ideas, include more information, or leave out some information. At this stage, now that you know exactly what you are going to include in your presentation, you can plan the introduction and conclusion. Then, when you are satisfied with the development of the different parts of your presentation, you can review the final form of your planning outline until you are very familiar with all of the information you want to present. You can look at Sample Worksheet 5 on page 252 of Appendix I to see a sample planning outline.

ACTIVITY 10-C

_____

1. Work in small groups. Your group may choose or be assigned several of the following topics. For each topic: (a) choose the best pattern of organization and (b) develop a skeleton outline of the body of the presentation:
    A. reasons that the Arctic should be opened to exploration by gas companies
    B. some solutions to the problem of ivory poaching in Africa
    C. ways that science education in secondary schools can be improved
    D. how archaeologists determine the age of an object
    E. how a periscope works
    F. the main causes of tides
    G. a description of an electroscope
    H. a comparison of computer X and computer Y
    I. how work is progressing on a current research project
    J. advantages and disadvantages of using irradiation to preserve food
    K. an explanation of the problem of mercury poisoning
    L. a description of the design of a new three-story factory
    M. the best way to save endangered species of plants
2. When all the groups have finished, compare your results.

E. Preparing Presentation Notes

Since your planning outline is very detailed, you will not be able to refer to it easily while you are speaking. However, you can use this outline to write brief presentation notes on small index or note cards. If you write on only one side of the cards, they will be easy for you to handle and refer to while you are talking. Your notes should be made up of key words or short phrases to help you remember the order of the important points you want to present. These notes should be written neatly and clearly so that you will be able to read them easily. If you write too much on a card, you will not be able to refer to it conveniently. You should be so familiar with the material you are presenting that you only need to glance at these notes to refresh your memory. If you want to remind yourself to emphasize something in the presentation, you can underline it, write it in capital letters, or use a different color ink. Also, you can indicate when to present any visual aids if you are using them in your presentation. In writing these notes, you can use one note card for the introduction, one for each main idea of the body, and one for the conclusion. So that you don't lose your place, you should number these cards in the order that you will use them. You can look at Worksheet 6 on page 254 of Appendix I to see sample presentation notes.

Presentation Techniques

USING SUPPORTING MATERIALS

In developing your presentation, you need to choose relevant information to support your main points and subpoints. The amount and type of supporting materials you use will determine how effective your presentation will be. By using a variety of supporting materials, you will prove or clarify the points you want to make. Also, different kinds of supporting materials will add interest to your presentation. Here are some different types of supporting materials you can use in your presentation:

Definitions are explanations of what words or concepts mean. You should always define technical or specialized terms that the listeners may not understand. Make sure that your definitions are brief, clear, and in language that your listeners can understand.

Facts are true statements about reality that can be verified. They add authority to your presentation and make it more convincing. You need to get these facts from sources that are accurate, reliable, and up to date. If the facts you use are not generally known or may be in dispute, be sure to indicate the source and date of the information ("according to _____," or "as reported in _____").

Statistics are facts reported in numbers. They can help you prove a point, but you should use them with care. In general, round numbers and approximate figures are easier for listeners to understand. Listeners may also need an explanation of the statistics that you present. You don't want to make your statistics too complex or use more numbers than your listeners can grasp. Be sure to include the source and date of any statistics that you use.

Examples are specific instances that illustrate or clarify a point. You can make a general statement or subject more specific by referring to particular people, places, or events. General concepts are often more interesting when they are explained in terms of sample problems or typical incidents.

Descriptions are detailed explanations that give your listeners a verbal picture of a person, place, or object. In describing an object you might discuss what it looks like in terms of size, shape, color, and dimension. You might also describe what it is made of, what it does, or how it works.

Testimony or quotations are the words of experts or authorities that help support your point. These should be brief and to the point. Be sure to give credit to the source of your quote.

Anecdotes are brief, often amusing, stories that you can use to explain or emphasize a point. Listeners often remember something longer when you illustrate it with a personal story. Any story you use, of course, should be suitable to the background and experience of your listeners. Also, your story should not be so long and complicated that your listeners forget the point that you are trying to make.

Comparison and contrast are used to explain something unfamiliar to most of the listeners by comparing it to something already familiar to them. Comparisons emphasize similarities, while contrasts stress the differences between two related things. You may find comparisons especially helpful in explaining technical objects to a nontechnical audience. Here are some examples:

- It's about the size of an average postage stamp.
- It's as thin as a piece of notebook paper.
- It works like a filter.
- Under the old system . . . , while with the new system . . .

ACTIVITY 10-D

1. Work individually to develop a three- to five-minute presentation on a topic of your choice. Use at least three different types of supporting materials: definitions, facts, statistics, examples, descriptions, testimony, anecdotes, or comparison and contrast.
2. Now work in small groups. Take turns giving your presentations to the group. Take notes on the different types of support each speaker uses. After each presentation, discuss the types of support the speaker included. Did the speaker effectively support his or her ideas? Can you suggest other kinds of support that the speaker might have used?

Presentation Assignment 4

After studying the information in this unit, you can prepare a five- to seven-minute presentation to give to a group or to the entire class. Look at the presentation evaluation form on page 159 to see how you will be evaluated. If you need guidelines for preparing your presentation, you can use the Final Checklist for Preparing an Oral Presentation on page 257 in Appendix II.

Suggested Topics

1. Discuss reasons for and against something, giving a balanced view of the issue.

   Sample issues:
   solar energy
   genetic engineering
   heart transplantation
   using irradiation as a food preservative
   nuclear power
   space exploration
   animal experimentation
   multinational companies building factories in developing countries

2. Discuss reasons for and against something, supporting one side or the other.

   Sample topics: See sample topics in #1.

   Guidelines:
   First, present the side of the issue that you don't support and then present the side that you do support. Your argument will have more force if your listeners feel that you have dealt fairly with the opposing view.

3. Discuss an event in terms of its causes and effects, emphasizing the causes.

   Sample events:
   mercury poisoning in a particular area
   land erosion in a particular area
   desertification in a particular area
   coronary heart disease
   acid rain

the "green revolution"
the construction of the Aswan High Dam
a particular nuclear accident (such as Chernobyl or Three Mile Island)
the Industrial Revolution
lowering the speed limit to 100 kilometers per hour in a particular country

4. Discuss an event in terms of its causes and effects, emphasizing the effects.

   Sample events: See sample events listed in #3.

5. Give a presentation based on one of the assignments listed for Unit 4 or Unit 7. Choose a type of presentation different from one you have already given.

Suggested Assignments for Listeners

The instructor may assign different students to do some of the following listening assignments. The listeners should then turn in their assignments to the instructor, give them to the speaker, or discuss their results with the rest of the group or class, according to the teacher's instructions.

1. Fill out the evaluation form.
2. Write two questions to ask the speaker after the presentation.
3. Identify the different types of support the speaker uses to develop the main ideas of the presentation: definitions, facts, statistics, examples, description, quotations, anecdotes, or comparison. Did the speaker effectively support the main points of the presentation?
4. Pay particular attention to the organization of the presentation. Consider the following questions in analyzing the organization:
   A. What was the central idea of the presentation?
   B. What pattern of organization did the speaker follow?
   C. What were the main points presented by the speaker?
   D. Were the main points presented in a logical way?
5. Pay particular attention to the speaker's language. Consider the following questions in analyzing the strengths and weaknesses of the speaker's ability to communicate:

A. Was the speaker able to precisely convey the message in terms of grammar? Did grammar problems interfere with the speaker's message at any time?

B. Was the speaker able to precisely convey the message in terms of vocabulary? Did vocabulary problems interfere with the speaker's message at any time?

C. Was the speaker's pronunciation clear?

Presentation Evaluation 4

Speaker: _____

Topic: _____

Evaluator: _____

Rating System
Complete the following evaluation form by filling in the appropriate number of points in the blanks provided. The point values are as follows:

2 = Excellent   1 = Satisfactory   0 = Needs Improvement

These points can be added up to give a total score for each section on the form. Follow your teacher's instructions in rating the speaker on one, some, or all of the sections included in this form. Space is provided on the form for your comments on specific strengths or weaknesses of the speaker's presentation. You can also add suggestions for improving future presentations.

I. *Delivery*

Points out of 10: _____   *Comments:*

_____ A. volume—loud enough
         to be heard clearly
_____ B. eye contact with audi-
         ence
_____ C. natural delivery—not
         read or memorized
_____ D. rate of speech—not too
         fast or too slow
_____ E. posture/body move-
         ment—no distracting
         mannerisms

II. *Content*

Points out of 10: _____   *Comments:*

_____ A. clear central idea
_____ B. topic suitable for time
          available—not too
          limited or too general
_____ C. topic suitable for this
          audience—not too
          technical or too
          well-known
_____ D. topic developed with
          relevant details, facts,
          examples that provide
          strong support of central
          idea
_____ E. presentation meets time
          requirements—not too
          long or too short

III. *Organization*

Points out of 10: _____   *Comments:*

_____ A. introduction
_____ B. use of transitions
_____ C. main points clearly
          stated
_____ D. development of ideas
          logical, easy to follow
_____ E. conclusion

IV. *Language*

Points out of 6: _____   *Comments:*

_____ A. accuracy of
          communication—clarity
          of ideas

_____ B. vocabulary appropriate
for this audience—
difficult or technical
words explained
_____ C. pronunciation/intonation

Total Number of Points Received by Speaker: _____

Total Number of Possible Points: _____

Questions to ask the speaker:

1. _____

2. _____

Analyzing Solutions 2

Expressions

This unit focuses on asking about and analyzing solutions (suggestions, proposals, plans, actions, rules, regulations, or laws) according to three possible criteria: feasibility, acceptability, and effectiveness. In a discussion, group members question, support, and/or oppose possible solutions with these and other criteria in mind. Before going over the expressions provided, you may want to discuss each function and then work individually or in small groups to list expressions that you are already familiar with. You can compare them with the ones listed here and then put a plus sign (+) next to those expressions that support and a minus sign (−) next to those that oppose a solution. As usual, the expressions listed are only some of the many possible ways of conveying each idea, so you may want to add other expressions or points to those included here.

Asking about feasibility

How $\left\{ \begin{array}{l} \text{feasible} \\ \text{workable} \\ \text{practical} \end{array} \right\}$ is this solution?

How easy will it be to implement this solution?

Is the required $\left\{ \begin{array}{l} \text{technology} \\ \text{equipment} \end{array} \right\}$ available?

Are the required $\left\{ \begin{array}{l} \text{resources} \\ \text{personnel} \\ \text{facilities} \end{array} \right\}$ available?

Analyzing feasibility

It's
It isn't
} {
feasible.
workable.
practical.
}

It's
It isn't
} worth the effort.

It will be {
easy
simple
} to put into effect.

It will be too {
much trouble
complicated
difficult
} to put into effect.

It will definitely work.

It won't work because we
don't have the necessary {
technology.
equipment.
resources.
personnel.
facilities.
}

Asking about acceptability

Will everyone involved {
be satisfied with
accept
} this solution?

Will the people in charge agree to this solution?

Analyzing acceptability

Everyone
Not everyone
} will {
be satisfied with
accept
} this solution.

The people in charge
Management
} {
will
won't
} agree to this decision.

Asking about effectiveness

Will this solution {
really solve the problem?
eliminate the causes of the problem?
}

Analyzing effectiveness

The solution {
will
won't
} be effective because _____.

The solution may not totally solve the problem,

but $\left\{\begin{array}{l}\text{it will certainly improve the situation.}\\ \text{it's a step in the right direction.}\\ \text{it's the best we can do for now.}\end{array}\right.$

Listening Practice

The following exercises can be completed by listening to Unit 11 on the tape.

Section 1.   There are two short discussions in this section, each on a different subject. Each discussion is broken into numbered segments.

A.   Listen to Section 1 on the tape. Check [✔] the criterion used to analyze each solution.

Solutions	Criteria		
	Feasibility	*Acceptability*	*Effectiveness*
Discussion One			
1. landfills	_____	_____	_____
2. incinerators	_____	_____	_____
3. recycling	_____	_____	_____
Discussion Two			
1. poison-control centers	_____	_____	_____
2. warnings on bottles	_____	_____	_____
3. safe packaging	_____	_____	_____
4. child-proof caps	_____	_____	_____

B.   Work with a partner, in a small group, or as a class to compare your answers.

Section 2.   There is one discussion in this section, broken into numbered segments. Scientists are discussing the destruction of the ozone layer. They believe that chlorofluorocarbons (CFCs) are a major cause of this problem.

A. Listen to Section 2 on the tape. Check [✓] the criterion used to analyze each solution.

Solutions	Criteria		
	Feasibility	Acceptability	Effectiveness
1. ban production in this country	_____	_____	_____
2. put an immediate worldwide ban on production	_____	_____	_____
3. phase out use over a two-year period	_____	_____	_____
4. freeze current levels of production	_____	_____	_____

B. Work with a partner, in a small group, or as a class to compare your answers.

C. Listen again. Decide whether the second speaker supports or opposes each solution. Put a check [✓] in the correct space and then write the expression that the speaker uses.

	Support	Oppose	Expressions
1.	_____	_____	_____
2.	_____	_____	_____
3.	_____	_____	_____
4.	_____	_____	_____

D. Work with a partner, in a small group, or as a class to compare your answers.

Controlled Practice

Exercise 1. Use a variety of expressions from the unit in discussing the illustrations on page 167.

Student A: Explain the problem depicted in the picture.
Student B: Offer a possible solution.
Student A: Ask a question about the solution.
Student B: Answer with any reasonable response.

Exercise 2.   Each of the following is a technical problem with many possible solutions. One solution for each problem is offered in the exercise. This solution may have many advantages or it may have many disadvantages, according to the criteria in this unit. Analyze each solution to determine its strengths and weaknesses by using appropriate expressions from the unit. You may also want to use the criteria and expressions presented in Unit 9 in analyzing these solutions.

Student A: Explain the problem and offer the given solution.

Student B: Ask a question about the solution.

Student A: Answer the question with any reasonable response.

Student C: Ask another question.

Student A: Answer the question.

General Interest

1. *Problem:*   Hunters kill millions of animals each year, leaving parts of the country without wildlife.
   Solution: The government should forbid all hunting.
2. *Problem:*   An active earthquake fault runs under a nuclear weapons development center. An earthquake could send plutonium and other radioactive substances over the densely populated area near the center.
   Solution: The center should be closed immediately.
3. *Problem:*   Farmers in a developing country do not allow their fields to lie fallow long enough. Consequently, yields have fallen and the soil is exhausted.
   Solution: The government should provide free ploughs so that deeper layers of soil can be turned up.

Science

4. *Problem:*   Fish have died in more than 200 lakes in one region because of acid rain.
   Solution: Anti-pollution devices should be required on all factory smokestacks.
5. *Problem:*   Energy consumption in a country has increased greatly in the last few years.
   Solution: Electric companies should raise the cost of electricity.
6. *Problem:*   A country faces the problem of agricultural surpluses due to over-production.
   Solution: The government can tax fertilizers and pesticides to reduce crop yields.

Solutions?

What about Feasibility?   Acceptability?   Effectiveness?

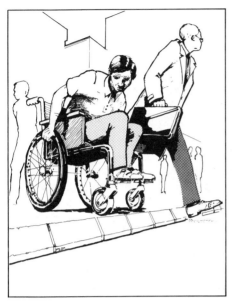

1. problems of the handicapped

2. crowded conditions in a public
   health clinic

3. water pollution

Engineering

 7. *Problem:* Government regulations have made it increasingly difficult for a company to dispose of toxic waste.

    Solution: The company can invest in research in an effort to reduce the amount of waste.

 8. *Problem:* People have been complaining that concerts in the local theater are ruined by echoes.

    Solution: Curtains and carpets can be added to absorb unwanted sound.

 9. *Problem:* A nuclear reactor is to be retired. The government must determine the best way to dismantle it.

    Solution: The reactor should be buried in concrete.

Health

10. *Problem:* Nursing is considered a low-status occupation. Therefore, few people become nurses.

    Solution: A national advertising campaign should be organized to upgrade the status of nursing.

11. *Problem:* A hospital is facing a serious problem with cross-contamination among inpatients.

    Solution: The hospital can provide isolation facilities.

12. *Problem:* Health clinics are giving antibiotics to patients who do not have bacterial infections.

    Solution: The Ministry of Health should set strict guidelines governing antibiotic prescriptions.

Exercise 3.   Go back to the previous exercise. This time think of your own solution to each problem.

    Student A: Explain the problem and suggest your own solution.

    Student B: Ask a question about the solution.

    Student A: Answer the question with any reasonable response.

    Student C: Ask another question.

    Student A: Answer the question.

Communication Concepts

GROUP TASK ROLES

Discussion groups are usually formed to accomplish a specific goal or task. The task may be for the group to solve a problem, to decide on a new policy, or to agree on a recommendation. In order for the group to be successful, each group member must understand the task and take a role in getting that task done. When a participant contributes ideas to the discussion that help the group to achieve its goal, that person is taking on a task role. Here are some important task roles:

1. *Initiating ideas or suggestions*

   Initiators suggest new ideas or actions. By bringing up new ideas for the group to discuss, initiators help the group to be more creative.

2. *Questioning*

   Questioners ask for facts, opinions, ideas, and suggestions from others. This improves group interaction and encourages other members to participate.

3. *Giving information or opinions*

   In this role, a group member offers facts or opinions that are relevant to the problem under discussion.

4. *Clarifying ideas*

   Clarifiers work to clear up possible confusion. They may clarify ideas by asking for clarification, paraphrasing comments, or explaining unclear remarks.

5. *Evaluating*

   Evaluators judge the ideas and suggestions of the group to see how practical, economical, logical, or fair they are. Evaluators may try to explain the advantages or disadvantages of the suggestion being discussed.

6. *Summarizing*

   Summarizers pull together and summarize the various ideas that have been offered. By checking to see whether the group members have reached agreement on a particular point, summarizers help keep the group working toward the goal.

7. *Elaborating*

Elaborators give examples or point out possible consequences of suggested solutions to show how they would actually work out if adopted by the group.

8. *Comparing*

A group member may try to compare or show relationships among various ideas or solutions that have been suggested by the group. This helps the group select the best solution.

Effective group members take on many of these task roles during a group discussion. That is, they contribute relevant information, ask questions, elaborate, clarify, evaluate, compare, or do whatever is needed in order to help the group accomplish its goal.

Discussion Techniques

CORRECTING YOURSELF

Sometimes you realize that another member of the discussion group has misunderstood or misinterpreted something you have said. It is also possible that you said something that you didn't really mean. For instance, you might have gotten your words mixed up or accidentally used a wrong word. In any case, you will have to correct yourself to clear up any possible confusion. You may want to use one of the following comments to explain:

Actually, that's not what I $\left\{ \begin{array}{l} \text{said.} \\ \text{meant.} \end{array} \right.$

I'm afraid you misunderstood me.

You must have misunderstood me.

Actually, what I $\left\{ \begin{array}{l} \text{said} \\ \text{meant} \end{array} \right\}$ was _____.

Discussion Practice

SOLVING A PROBLEM

The cases in this section will give you further practice in participating in problem-solving discussions.

Instructions

1. Refer to the detailed instructions included in the Discussion Practice section of Unit 2 for guidance in choosing cases, getting organized, brainstorming, selecting ideas, preparing for, and starting the discussion.
2. Group observers should complete the Observer Evaluation Form on page 175 as directed by the instructor. They can then discuss their evaluations with the group members. If other groups have worked on the same case, compare your solutions.

CASE 1: WOMEN IN TECHNOLOGY

Situation

A developing country is in urgent need of trained technicians, even though these jobs are relatively highly paid. The Minister of Education believes that women are a possible source of the needed labor. Although the majority of women work, very few work in nontraditional fields, such as metallurgy or physics. In fact, only 10 percent of workers in science-related fields are females. The government has called a meeting to discuss the situation.

Purpose of the Discussion

Group members should try to agree on the best way to encourage women to take up careers in science.

Group Roles

The following people take part in the discussion:

> Leader: a representative of the government
> Representative(s) of the Ministry of Education
> Trained technician(s) in science-related fields
> Representative(s) of women working in traditional fields

CASE 2: ADDING SULFITES TO FOOD

Situation

Many restaurants in one community add sulfiting agents to their fresh fruits and vegetables. This keeps the food from discoloring, and thus makes it more attractive to their customers. Some customers, however, have complained. They say that sulfites are not necessary. They believe that people should eat fresh food, not chemically preserved food. Moreover, sulfites can cause faintness, shortness of breath, and other allergic reactions, especially in those suffering from asthma. These customers want the restaurants to stop using sulfites. Restaurant owners have refused. They say that sulfites are not harmful to the general public. Furthermore, their use avoids waste and keeps prices low. The government has been asked to settle the dispute. A meeting has been called to discuss the issue.

Purpose of the Discussion

Group members should try to agree on the best policy regarding the use of sulfites in restaurant food.

Group Roles

The following people take part in the discussion:

> Leader: a representative of the government
> Representative(s) of the restaurants
> Customer(s)

CASE 3: CHEMICAL PLANT LEAK

Situation

After years of investigations and legal disputes, next month a multinational chemical firm plans to reopen its plant in a developing country. The plant was shut down 5 years ago when poisonous vapor escaped from a storage tank, killing more than 500 people and injuring thousands. A citizens' group has asked the government to keep the plant from reopening. Citizens say that the plant should remain closed until the community can be assured that the plant can be operated safely. Plant representatives say that safety features have been installed and the accident cannot happen again. A meeting has been called to discuss the situation.

Purpose of the Discussion

Group members should try to agree on the best action to take regarding the chemical plant.

Group Roles

The following people take part in the discussion:

> Leader: a representative of the government
> Representative(s) of the chemical firm
> Representative(s) of the citizens' group

CASE 4: HEALTH FEES

Situation

The Ministry of Finance has proposed that the government charge fees for health services. A representative of this ministry says that people are misusing or taking advantage of the free public medical care provided to all residents. Because services are free, many people go to public clinics with minor or even imaginary problems. Many health professionals are opposed to the Ministry's proposal. They believe that all people have a right to free health care. Residents, too, are against the proposal, since they feel that health charges place a large financial burden on people with limited incomes. A meeting has been called to discuss the issue.

Purpose of the Discussion

Group members should try to agree on the best way to provide quality health care to residents.

Group Roles

The following people take part in the discussion:

Leader: a representative of the government
Representative(s) of the Ministry of Finance
Health professional(s)
Resident(s)

Discussion Evaluation

OBSERVER EVALUATION FORM

   1. *Identifying the group*

    A. Discussion topic: _____

    B. Names of students in group: _____

    _____

   2. *Listening to the discussion.* On a separate sheet of paper write the first two possible solutions that the group members discuss. As each one is analyzed, make a list of the different questions that the participants ask.

   3. *Evaluating the discussion.* After writing the questions, put a check [✔] in the column to indicate which of the following points the participants discussed:

	Solution 1	*Solution 2*
A. cost	_____	_____
B. time	_____	_____
C. side effects	_____	_____
D. feasibility	_____	_____
E. acceptability	_____	_____
F. effectiveness	_____	_____

   4. *Rating the discussion.* Use the following scales to rate the discussion group:

    A. *Problem Solving.* Did the discussion move in an organized, logical way toward the final decision?

Excellent	Satisfactory	Weak	Unsatisfactory
3	2	1	0

    |_____|_____|_____|_____

    B. *Leader Control.* Did the leader effectively guide the discussion, not taking too much or too little control?

Excellent	Satisfactory	Weak	Unsatisfactory
3	2	1	0

    |_____|_____|_____|_____

Considering Consequences

Expressions

The following list includes only some of the many possible expressions that are used to convey each function. Space is provided for you to add other expressions related to each function as you work through the unit. Before going over the lists provided, you may want to discuss each function and then work individually or in small groups to list expressions that you are already familiar with. You can then identify any expressions that seem to be particularly formal, informal, direct, or indirect and then compare them with those listed here. You might also discuss possible situations in which these expressions could appropriately be used.

Asking about possible consequences

$$\text{What} \begin{Bmatrix} \text{will} \\ \text{might} \\ \text{may} \\ \text{could} \end{Bmatrix} \text{happen if} \begin{cases} \text{the factory closes down?} \\ \text{public transportation is improved?} \\ \text{researchers are careless?} \end{cases}$$

Predicting possible consequences

$$\text{If} \begin{Bmatrix} \text{the factory closes} \\ \text{down,} \\ \text{public transportation is} \\ \text{improved,} \\ \text{researchers are care-} \\ \text{less,} \end{Bmatrix} \text{then} \begin{cases} \text{many people will lose} \\ \text{their jobs.} \\ \text{more people might} \\ \text{use it.} \\ \text{experimental results} \\ \text{may not be accurate.} \end{cases}$$

$$\text{Unless}\begin{cases} \text{the forest fire is put} \\ \quad \text{out,} \\ \text{people conserve elec-} \\ \quad \text{tricity,} \\ \text{more students go into} \\ \quad \text{physics,} \end{cases}\begin{cases} \text{hundreds of people may} \\ \quad \text{die.} \\ \text{the electric company will} \\ \quad \text{raise the rates.} \\ \text{the country will face a} \\ \quad \text{shortage of physicists.} \end{cases}$$

Asking about alternatives

$$\text{What other alternatives}\begin{cases} \text{can you think of?} \\ \text{do you see?} \\ \text{are there?} \end{cases}$$

Are there any other possibilities?

Expressing possibility

$$\left.\begin{array}{l} \text{Perhaps} \\ \text{Maybe} \end{array}\right\} \underline{\hspace{3cm}}.$$

It's possible that _____.

Listening Practice

The following exercises can be completed by listening to Unit 12 on the tape.

Section 1. There are eight short dialogs in this section. Each one is about a different subject.

A. Look at the following actions. What might happen if these actions occur? Before listening to the dialogs, work individually or with a partner to think of one possible consequence of each action. Write this consequence on line "A."

1. Unless we stop the rapid increase of the world population, ...

A. _____

B. _____

2. If the destruction of the rain forests continues, ...

A. _____

B. _____

3. If the government passes a law requiring everyone to wear seat-belts, ...

   A. _____

   B. _____

4. If an artificial playing surface is used on a football field, ...

   A. _____

   B. _____

5. If a plant doesn't get enough light, ...

   A. _____

   B. _____

6. Unless we cut down on the emission of greenhouse gases, ...

   A. _____

   B. _____

7. If authorities close the center of the city to all traffic, ...

   A. _____

   B. _____

8. If medical researchers can't get enough patients to participate in clinical trials, ...

   A. _____

   B. _____

B. Now listen to Section 1 on the tape. If the speaker mentions the same consequence that you have written, put a check [✓] next to it. If the speaker presents a different idea, write it on line "B."

C. Work with a partner, in a small group, or as a class to compare your answers.

Section 2. There is one discussion in this section. Several officials of the Wildlife Refuge Center are evaluating possible operating policies of the refuges.

A. Look at the following ideas. What might be some possible consequences of these actions? Before listening to the discussion, work individually or with a partner to think of one possible consequence of each action. Write this consequence on line "A."

1. If the refuges are closed to the public, ...

    A. _____

    B. _____

2. If camping is permitted everywhere in the parks, ...

    A. _____

    B. _____

3. If fishing is permitted in the sanctuaries, ...

    A. _____

    B. _____

4. If people are allowed to hunt in the parks, ...

    A. _____

    B. _____

5. If hunting is banned in the refuges, ...

    A. _____

    B. _____

6. If the wildlife parks restrict visitors' activities, ...

    A. _____

    B. _____

7. If all visitors to the refuges pay an entrance fee, ...

    A. _____

    B. _____

8. If the sanctuaries allow lumbering, ...

    A. _____

    B. _____

B. Now listen to Section 2 on the tape. If one of the speakers mentions the same consequence that you have written, put a check [✔] next to it. If a speaker presents a different idea, write it on line "B."

C. Work with a partner, in a small group, or as a class to compare your answers.

Controlled Practice

Exercise 1. Try to use some different expressions from the unit in discussing the illustrations on page 182.

> *Students:* Suggest possible consequences of these actions.

Exercise 2. The following are actions that might happen.

> *Student A:* Ask Student B about a possible consequence of the action (using the correct verb form).
>
> *Student B:* Predict a possible consequence.
>
> *Student A:* Ask about an alternative consequence.
>
> *Student C:* · Predict another possible consequence.

1. member of a research team/publish false data
2. farmers/use less fertilizer
3. doctors/advertise their services
4. adequate lubrication in a machine/not maintained
5. level of the oceans/rise by one or two meters
6. number of rabies cases/increase suddenly
7. company/require mandatory AIDS testing
8. a hospital/cannot get enough organ donors
9. littering/continue
10. more ultraviolet light/reach the earth
11. swarm of locusts/move into an area
12. government/cut funds for space exploration
13. a company/experience a chemical leak
14. people/doubt that a vaccine is safe
15. athletes/use anabolic steroids

Exercise 3. Use a variety of expressions from the unit to discuss possible consequences.

> *Student A:* Complete the sentence in any appropriate way.
>
> *Student B:* Complete the sentence in another appropriate way.

General

1. If speed limits are reduced to 50 m.p.h., _____.

2. Energy consumption will continue to increase unless _____.

3. The government might cut funds for scientific research if _____.

4. If smoking is banned in all public places, _____.

5. Unless universities can attract outstanding science professors, _____.

6. If scarce natural resources are not preserved, _____.

7. Air pollution might be controlled if _____.

8. Many species of animals will become extinct unless _____.

9. If a plastic dome is put over the Acropolis, _____.

10. There will continue to be a shortage of women in the field of science and technology unless _____.

Science

11. If desertification continues, _____.

12. Whales will continue to be killed illegally unless _____.

13. Unless the government controls genetic engineering, _____.

14. If tropical rain forests continue to be developed, _____.

15. Drinking water may be contaminated if _____.

Engineering

16. If scientists are able to predict the paths of oil slicks, _____.

17. Electric cars might become popular if _____.

18. Unless companies learn how to dispose of toxic wastes safely, _____.

19. If rubbish is used as a source of energy, _____.

20. A bridge might collapse if _____.

Medicine

21. If nurses are allowed to prescribe medicine, _____.

22. An epidemic of cholera might occur if _____.

23. Unless a cure for cancer is found, _____.

24. The cost of medical care will continue to increase unless _____.

25. Parents might not get their children immunized against polio if _____.

1. automating a factory

2. building skyscrapers

3. conducting mass immunizations

4. building dams

Communication Concepts

GROUP BUILDING ROLES

As people work together to solve a problem, they have to deal with both the problem and the other members of the group. Task roles, which deal with *what* the group is doing, are clearly important. However, other important roles are related to *how* the members feel about working in the group. In order for a group to be effective, the members should enjoy working with each other. When group interaction occurs in a supportive atmosphere, people feel that they have something important to contribute to the group. Participants show respect for the ideas of others. This attitude keeps communication open throughout the discussion. Thus, group members are able to work effectively toward a solution to the problem under discussion.

In order for the group to function well, there are certain group building roles that participants need to perform. These group building roles help people feel good about participating in the group. In a successful group discussion all of the members should feel responsible for taking whatever role is necessary to keep the group interacting in a positive way. Here are some common group building roles:

1. *Encouraging*

   Group members encourage others by showing an interest in their ideas and suggestions. They may ask questions or make comments such as "Good idea" in response to other people's ideas.

2. *Gate keeping*

   Gate keepers help to "keep the gate open" in a discussion by making sure that everyone has a chance to speak. They may try to bring in quiet members or to control people who talk too much. Gate keepers work to keep communication open.

3. *Harmonizing*

   Harmonizers try to keep everyone satisfied during a discussion by solving any disagreements or conflicts that occur. They may try to help a difficult situation by joking or suggesting a break.

4. *Compromising*

   Compromisers try to help the group find acceptable solutions to a problem by finding areas of agreement. They may admit that they are wrong or offer to change their position in order to go along with the other members.

5. *Coaching*

Coaches try to help other members who are having trouble expressing their ideas. For example, a coach might help a member who cannot think of the correct word to use.

By taking on these group building roles, group members help to maintain a positive, supportive atmosphere that improves a group's performance.

Discussion Techniques

KEEPING THE DISCUSSION MOVING

It is usually the group leader's responsibility to keep the discussion moving. Of course, the leader must be careful not to cut off discussion of a point too soon. However, when group members start repeating the same idea or it seems that the discussion is not getting anywhere, the leader should move the discussion on to the next point. Even if members cannot reach agreement, discussion of a particular point should not go on too long. The following comments can be used to keep the discussion moving:

I think we'd better go on to another point.

To bring up another point, _____.

I think we've covered this point. Let's move on to something else.

Let's go on to the next point.

I think we've spent enough time on this point. Why don't we go on to another issue?

Are there any more comments before we move on to the next point?

Discussion Practice

SOLVING A PROBLEM

The cases in this section will give you further practice in participating in problem-solving discussions.

Instructions

1. Refer to the detailed instructions included in the Discussion Practice section of Unit 2 for guidance in choosing cases, getting organized, brainstorming, selecting ideas, preparing for, and starting the discussion.
2. Group observers should complete the Observer Evaluation Form on page 189 as directed by the instructor. They can then discuss their evaluations with the group members. If other groups have worked on the same case, compare your solutions.

CASE 1: SCIENTIFIC INTEGRITY

Situation

The head of a research team has publicly announced that the team has made a major scientific discovery. Rival research teams have been working hard for the past few years to be the first to make this discovery, so the announcement has received a lot of public attention. However, the truth is that the team's hypothesis has not yet been confirmed. Further tests are needed. The head of the team believes the announcement was necessary for the team to maintain its reputation for leadership in the field. This step will ensure continued funding of their research. The other team members oppose the action. They believe it was unethical to make this premature announcement. A director of the research company has called a meeting to discuss the situation.

Purpose of the Discussion

Group members should try to agree on the best action to take in response to the team leader's announcement.

Group Roles

The following people take part in the discussion:

> Leader: a director of the research company
> The head of the research team
> Member(s) of the research team

CASE 2: GREEN BELTS

Situation

Dust storms are a continual problem for a large city located in a desert area. Botanists from the Academy of Natural Science want the government to plant trees, bushes, and grass in various parts of the city. The scientists say that such green belts will reduce the sandstorms. Government officials, however, say that such a project is too expensive for the government to undertake alone. Officials want the city's residents to be involved. A meeting has been called to discuss the situation.

Purpose of the Discussion

Group members should try to agree on the best way to create green belts in the city.

Group Roles

The following people take part in the discussion:

> Leader: a representative of the government
> Botanist(s)
> Resident(s)

CASE 3: INNER-CITY IMPROVEMENT

Situation

Abandoned buildings, burned-out structures, and garbage-littered streets surround the central business district of one major city. As residents have moved to the suburbs, the inner city has badly deteriorated. To attract people back to the city and to reclaim the area, urban planners want to construct a high-density housing project. Such a project will combine businesses, recreational space, and residential areas in several high-rise buildings. City engineers also favor this high-rise housing project. They say that concentrating housing units in one structure will decrease construction costs and thus lower rents.

Residents of the area disagree, however. They believe that crime may increase with such a large concentration of people. They say that people need the open spaces of single-family units. The government has called a meeting to discuss the situation.

Purpose of the Discussion

Group members should try to agree on the best way to improve the inner city.

Group Roles

The following people take part in the discussion:

> Leader: a representative of the government
> Urban planner(s)
> Resident(s)

CASE 4: PILOTS ON DRUGS

Situation

Medical personnel are concerned about the increasing number of pilots who have been receiving treatment for cocaine abuse at local hospitals and rehabilitation clinics. The physicians and nurses are forbidden by law from reporting a pilot's drug abuse to the airline or to the Federal Aviation Administration (FAA). Furthermore, pilots say that they will seek treatment for drug abuse only if they are assured of their right to confidential treatment. Although most physicians and nurses believe strongly in the importance of patient confidentiality laws, they also feel frustrated by these laws because they feel a moral obligation to protect the public from potential accidents caused by impaired pilots. FAA officials believe that they are protecting public safety by following a strict policy that requires the permanent grounding of any pilot found to be using drugs. Also, commercial pilots are required to undergo extensive physical examinations every six months. FAA-certified physicians who conduct these examinations are required to report any suspected or proven abuse of alcohol or drugs. Physicians complain, however, that testing for drug use or abuse is not permitted in these examinations. A government investigator has called a meeting to discuss the situation.

Purpose of the Discussion

Group members should try to agree on the best way to deal with the problem of drug abuse by pilots.

Group Roles

The following people take part in the discussion:

Leader: the government investigator
Representative(s) of the pilots
Representative(s) of medical personnel
FAA official(s)

Discussion Evaluation

OBSERVER EVALUATION FORM

1. *Listening to an individual.* In this discussion you should observe only one speaker.

   A. Speaker's name/role: _____

   B. Topic of discussion: _____

2. *Evaluating the speaker.* As you listen to the discussion, notice whether the speaker takes on any group building roles: (a) encouraging, (b) gate keeping, (c) harmonizing, (d) compromising, or (e) coaching. Write the comments/questions you hear that support positive group interaction and then later you can decide which type of group building role each seems to be:

Remarks/Questions	*Group Building Roles*

3. *Rating the speaker.* As directed by your instructor, use one, some, or all of the following scales to rate the speaker:

   A. *Interaction.* Did the speaker effectively interact with others? Use a variety of functions? Initiate? Involve others? Ask questions?

Excellent	Satisfactory	Weak	Unsatisfactory
3	2	1	0

B. *Use of Expressions.* Did the speaker effectively and accurately use a variety of expressions?

Excellent	Satisfactory	Weak	Unsatisfactory
3	2	1	0

C. *Content.* Did the speaker contribute logical, relevant information and ideas? Stay on the subject? Analyze solutions? Show strong support of arguments?

Excellent	Satisfactory	Weak	Unsatisfactory
3	2	1	0

D. *Accuracy.* Did the speaker communicate ideas clearly with effective control of grammar, vocabulary, and pronunciation?

Excellent	Satisfactory	Weak	Unsatisfactory
3	2	1	0

Using Visual Aids

Presentation Preparation

USING VISUAL AIDS

A. Types of Visual Aids

In preparing your presentation, you should consider using visual aids to clarify complex ideas or to emphasize important points. Visual aids help people understand and remember the information you are presenting because they involve the listeners' sense of sight as well as sound. Visual aids also increase the listeners' interest in your subject and help keep their attention focused on your ideas. When you select visual materials for your presentation, you have to decide which of the following types are best for your purpose, your listeners, and the physical setting.

Boards, such as blackboards (chalkboards) or whiteboards, are commonly used as visual aids. They are extremely useful for writing down simple information such as names, dates, or technical words. Also, you can draw your own diagrams or pictures as you need them.

Flip charts are inexpensive pads of oversized paper. You use a flip chart in the same way as you use the blackboard, except that you flip pages over instead of erasing the material. Since flip charts are rather small, you can use them effectively only in a very small room.

Charts are used to represent information in a graphic way. Charts are usually made of large pieces of very stiff paper or cardboard so they are easy to handle and display. Charts may display diagrams, flow charts, organizational charts, line graphs, bar graphs, and pie graphs. These are especially useful in conveying technical or statistical data in an accurate and understandable manner.

Objects can make good visual aids if they are large enough for everyone in the audience to see and small enough for you to be able to carry around.

Models are representations of actual objects. They are especially useful in describing or explaining parts of the body or engines, bridges, and other structures.

Photographs and pictures are not usually effective visual aids since they are often too small to be seen by everyone in the audience.

Overhead projectors can be used both for small and large groups. The major advantage of this type of projector is that you can face the audience while you are using it and you do not have to darken the room to get a clear image. Although this type of projector requires you to transfer material onto transparencies, these are quite easy to make.

Opaque projectors do not require any modification of the material to be projected onto the screen. You can use pictures from books or magazines. The major disadvantage of this type of projector is that you can only get a clear image by darkening the room. This often takes the focus off the speaker.

Films and slides can be very effective in presenting a message, although they tend to replace a presentation rather than supplement it. Because films and slides take attention away from the speaker, they are not usually considered to be effective visual aids.

Handouts are written supplements that you can give to people in the audience. Handouts have many purposes: to provide additional material that you do not have time to cover, to outline or summarize your main points, to present statistics, or to serve as worksheets. People in the audience often like handouts since they give them something to look at and also to take home for later reference. Although handouts may be popular with members of your audience, you should be aware that they can distract listeners from your presentation. While you are talking, people may be reading their handouts or looking around to see how they are being distributed.

B. Preparing Visual Aids

In order to choose or prepare effective visual aids, you should follow these guidelines:

1. Keep visual aids simple and clear. Obviously, people in the audience do not have much time to examine each visual aid in great detail.
2. Each visual aid should focus on only one idea. It is better to show several simple visual aids rather than to crowd too much information on one.
3. Consider the number of people in the audience and the size of the room in choosing or preparing visual aids. Make sure that the visual aid is large enough for everyone to see easily.
4. Visual aids need to be organized so that the audience can understand them quickly and easily. The audience will be confused by an overly detailed or technical visual aid. Be sure that your visual aids are aimed at the appropriate technical level of your listeners.
5. Visual aids should be neatly prepared with as few words as possible. It is essential for the lettering to be large and easy to read. Colors should be bright and in sharp contrast to the background.

C. General Guidelines for Using Visual Aids

Once you have prepared or obtained your visual aids, you need to consider how you will actually use them in your presentation. Here are some general guidelines:

1. Stand to the side when you present visual aids so that everyone in the audience can see them. You can use a pointer to refer to details so that your body does not block someone's view.
2. When you show your visual aid be sure to continue facing the listeners. You should be familiar enough with the visual aid that you do not have to keep looking at it in order to be able to explain it.
3. Limit the number of visual aids that you use. Since visual aids should emphasize important points, the use of too many will reduce their impact. Keep in mind that the purpose of your presentation is not to explain the visual aids.
4. Do not stop talking while you are showing the visual aid. You should explain and interpret the visual aid as you are showing it to the listeners.
5. Show each visual aid only when you are discussing it. Bring it out when you want people to look at it and then remove it when you move on to another point. People tend to look at visuals as long as they are in sight, and you want to keep the audience's attention focused on each point as it is presented.

6. Before your presentation make sure that the room has the necessary electrical outlets in the right place. Also, be sure that there is a blackboard (and chalk) if you plan to use a board.

D. Guidelines for Using Specific Visual Aids

In addition to the general guidelines presented for using visual aids, there are special considerations in using a few specific types of visual aids:

1. Boards

- Use the board only for writing simple information. Write at the board for a few seconds at a time.
- Plan in advance any information that you want to put on the board. Practice drawing any diagrams and be sure that you know the correct spelling of any words that you might write on the board.
- Do not cover the board with too much information.
- Keep your writing neat and straight. Make sure that everyone in the room can read what you have written. If you are not used to writing on the board, practice before you give your presentation.
- Keep your face toward the audience as much as possible when you are writing at the board. Do not talk to the board.
- Instead of planning to write much of your information on the board, you can consider using other types of visual aids to present this material. Visuals prepared in advance are generally clearer and better organized than something you write on the board while you are giving the presentation.

2. Flip Charts

- You can prepare some pages in advance.
- Do not put too much material on one page.
- Give the people in the audience enough time to look over the information on each page.
- Use bright colored markers.
- If you prepare some pages in advance, be sure that they are in the right order in the pad.

3. Overhead Projector

- Before you begin your presentation, make sure that you have the overhead projector in the right place for the size of image that you want to project. Check to see if everyone will be able to read what is written on the transparency.
- Plan your transparencies in advance. Make sure that you have them ready to use in the order that you want to present them.

4. Handouts

- Try to avoid distributing handouts while you are giving your presentation. People will be looking at the handouts instead of paying attention to you.
- Do not hand out too many pages of material or your listeners will not be able to sort out what is useful from what is not.
- Do not read the handout material to the audience.
- If possible, wait until the end of your presentation to distribute handouts.

ACTIVITY 13-A

1. Work in a small group. Review the following types of visual aids to make sure that all members of the group are familiar with them:

charts	flip charts
• a line graph	blackboards
• a bar graph	objects
• a pie graph	photographs
• an organizational chart	overhead projections
• a flowchart	handouts
• a diagram	slides or films

2. Continue working in the same groups. Consider the value of the above visual aids in clarifying, emphasizing, or adding interest to certain points of a presentation. Work on some or all of the following points, as directed by your instructor. Determine which of these visual aids would be best:

_____ A. to compare two makes of computers on the basis of price, size, type of disk drive, memory, and operating system

_____ B. to explain activities that teachers can use to motivate high school students

_____ C. to show the correct method of brushing your teeth

_____ D. to help explain the meanings of two technical terms

_____ E. to compare a spider and a scorpion

_____ F. to show how your department's workload has increased month by month during the past year

_____ G. to explain how coffee is freeze dried

_____ H. to show the breakdown of employees in your organization according to types of jobs

_____ I. to show the facilities of your company

_____ J. to provide a list of reference materials that listeners can use to get further information on your topic

_____ K. to show how sales of a product change each day over a period of a week

_____ L. to show the damage pollution has caused to a historic building

_____ M. to show the parts of an eye

_____ N. to compare two types of houseplants

_____ O. to show the structure of a DNA molecule

_____ P. to help listeners remember several important dates

_____ Q. to show the difference in income earned by men and women in several different professions

3. When all the groups have finished, compare your results.

Presentation Techniques

HANDLING QUESTIONS

Question-and-answer sessions are valuable because they give listeners a chance to become involved in your presentation. They are also useful in providing you with feedback on how well you communicated your information. Since it is important to make your listeners feel that you know your topic well, it is essential to be prepared to answer their questions. If you prepare carefully for your presentation, you should be able to answer most of the questions that people ask. Of course, you might be nervous about difficult questions that people could bring up. One way to deal with this is to think about these points as you are planning your presentation. You can then include the answers to these questions in the presentation, if possible. Here are some general guidelines to help you handle the question-and-answer session effectively:

1. Let your listeners know in advance when you want them to ask questions—as you go along or at the end of the presentation. In an impromptu situation, with only a few listeners, you should probably encourage people to ask questions as you go along. However, in giving an extemporaneous presentation you may find that questions disrupt your flow of thought and make it difficult for you to give an organized presentation. In this case, you can say, "I'll save some time at the end of my presentation for your questions. I'd appreciate it if you could save your questions and comments until then."

2. As you begin the question-and-answer session, set a definite time limit. This will help move things along and keep you from getting involved in long debates.

3. Make sure that you clearly understand the question that was asked. You might want to restate the question in your own words to clarify it for yourself and for the other listeners. You can say, "As I understand your question, you are asking _____."

4. Answer each question as fully as you can. At the same time, you should be brief and to the point. The question-and-answer period does not usually last long, and you want to give as many people as possible a chance to ask their questions.

5. If you do not know the answer to a question, say, "I'm afraid I don't have the answer to that question" or "I'm afraid I can't answer that." You are not expected to have the answer to every possible question, so don't worry. However, you might offer to find the answer for the listener. Show the listener that you are sincere by following up on your offer.

6. Be polite under all circumstances even if the questioner is rude or tries to put you in a difficult position. You cannot control what the questioner says, but you can control your reaction to it. Your first concern should be to keep the respect of the people who are listening to you.

7. Prepare your audience for the end of the question-and-answer session. You can signal the end of the session by saying, "I think we have time for one more question before bringing this to a close."

During the question-and-answer session people may ask you to clarify points you made or to give further information about something you brought up in your presentation. These kinds of questions should generally be easy for you to answer. However, some types of questions may give you some difficulty. The following activity will give you practice in answering some potentially difficult questions.

ACTIVITY 13-B

1. Imagine the following situation: You have just given a presentation to a group of people and now they are asking you questions. What do you think is the best thing to do or say in each of the following situations?
2. Work with a partner or in small groups. Write a possible response to each of the following situations on an "answer sheet."
   A. Instead of asking a question, the person strongly, rather angrily, disagrees with your point of view.
   B. Instead of asking a question, the person states his or her own viewpoints that agree with yours.
   C. The person states positively that some information you have given is inaccurate, but you are absolutely sure that you are correct.
   D. The person says that some information you have given is inaccurate, and you are not sure whether your information was correct or not.
   E. The person asks a question so basic that you realize that he or she did not understand any of your presentation.
   F. The person asks a question that will require a very long, complicated, or technical answer.
   G. The person asks a question totally unrelated to the information you have given in your presentation.
   H. The person tries to ask many questions when other people are waiting for their turn.
3. When another group has finished, exchange your "answer sheets" and compare your results.
4. Compare your responses with some suggested responses listed on page 202. Keep in mind, of course, that there are many possible ways of dealing with each situation, so the suggested responses are not necessarily the "right" answers.

ACTIVITY 13-C

1. Work individually to develop a three- to five-minute presentation on a topic of your choice.
2. Now work in small groups. Take turns giving your presentations to the group. As each person is speaking, prepare a number of questions, some of them designed to be difficult, for the speaker to answer at the end of the presentation.
3. If possible, tape record the question-and-answer session. The tape can be replayed at the end of the session for you to analyze the strengths and weaknesses of the speaker's answers. Then, work together to develop more effective answers to some of the questions.

Presentation Assignment 5

After studying the information in this unit, you can prepare a five- to seven-minute presentation to give to a group or to the entire class. Your instructor may assign a topic or allow you to choose your own. Look at the presentation evaluation form on page 204 to see how you will be evaluated. Your instructor will inform you whether or not you need to use a visual aid. If a visual aid is required, then you will have to choose a topic that lends itself to visual materials. If one is not required, then you will not be evaluated in that area. When preparing this presentation, you can refer to the Final Checklist for Preparing an Oral Presentation on page 257 in Appendix II.

Suggested Topics

1. Classify people or things into different categories.
   Sample topics:

   fungi
   satellites
   structural materials
   organs of the body
   dams
   engineers
   nuclear power plants
   mountains
   clouds
   insects

Guidelines:

A. The purpose of classifying things is to divide them into classes or categories in order to be able to understand them better.

B. Make the divisions by a single logical principle: function, purpose, size, material, source, location, type.

C. Choose categories that include all of the items that need to be classified.

D. Make sure that each item fits into only one category.

2. Compare and contrast two or three brands of a product that your department at work might need to buy. Recommend the best product to buy.

Sample products:
office computers
photocopiers
microscopes
typewriters
cameras
binoculars
slide projectors
company cars
telescopes
video cameras

Guidelines:

A. The purpose of a comparison/contrast presentation is to compare two related things by showing their similarities or differences. A comparison presentation concentrates on the similarities, while a contrast presentation focuses on the differences.

B. Evaluate the products in terms of cost, performance, quality, reliability, ease of use, durability.

C. Do a point-by-point comparison, mentioning one criterion and then discussing how Product A and Product B compare on this one point. Then go on to the next point and compare the two products.

D. A visual aid would help the audience see the comparison more clearly.

3. Compare and contrast two related objects or processes.

Sample topics:
a diesel and a gas engine
stars and planets
a refracting and a reflecting telescope
radar and sonar
viruses and bacteria
spiders and scorpions

        crocodiles and alligators
        exocrine and endocrine glands
        tendons and ligaments
        arteries and veins
        weathering and erosion
        freezing and flash evaporation to desalinate water

4. Compare and contrast two or three ways of solving a problem.

Guidelines:

    A. Evaluate the different courses of action in terms of effectiveness, cost, time, possible side effects, feasibility, acceptability, and fairness.

    B. A visual aid would help the audience see the comparison more clearly.

5. Hold a symposium with four or five students.

Sample topics:

        lack of quality medical care in developing countries
        ways that science can improve the quality of life
        using technology to end world hunger
        scarcity of world natural resources
        developing alternative sources of energy
        superconductivity

Guidelines:

    A. A symposium is a series of related presentations on different aspects of a particular subject or problem. This provides thorough and orderly coverage of a topic for an audience.

    B. Three to five participants divide the subject into different aspects or parts. Each of the participants then prepares a four- to five-minute presentation on the part he or she is responsible for.

    C. A moderator, sitting with the participants, is in charge of the symposium. The moderator should open the symposium and introduce each speaker.

    D. After the presentations the moderator may allow some time for the participants to interact with each other before opening the symposium up to questions from the audience.

    E. The moderator is responsible for closing the symposium.

6. Conduct a survey or administer a questionnaire and give a presentation on the results.

Guidelines:

    This assignment is appropriate only if you have the necessary background in conducting surveys or in developing and administering questionnaires.

POSSIBLE RESPONSES TO ACTIVITY 13-B

1. Listen politely and then restate your point of view, with additional evidence, if possible. Do not act annoyed or argue with the questioner. If the person repeats his or her position, you can say, "Well, we'll have to agree to disagree on this point," or "Unfortunately, there's no time to go into this more deeply right now."
2. Show the listeners how this person's ideas support your own point of view. You can say, "Yes, that fits in exactly with what I was saying."
3. If possible, give your source of information or provide additional support for your statement. If you cannot do so, you can say, "I believe that my information is correct, but I will certainly recheck my facts."
4. Do not feel threatened or regard this as an attack. You can say, "I appreciate your bringing this to my attention. I'll have to recheck my sources to see what is correct."
5. You can say, "Well, I don't think we have time to discuss that point right now, but I'll be happy to talk with you about it later."
6. Do not take up the entire question-and-answer period answering just one question. You can say, "That's an interesting question, but it would take much too long to answer it adequately. Perhaps we can discuss it later."
7. You can say, "That's an interesting question, but my presentation doesn't really deal with that issue," or "I'm afraid I don't see how that question applies to what I've said."
8. You can say, "I'm very pleased by your interest, but perhaps we should give others a chance to ask a few questions. I hope we can talk in more detail later."

Suggested Assignments for Listeners

The instructor may assign different students to do some of the following listening assignments. The listeners should then turn in their assignments to the instructor, give them to the speaker, or discuss their results with the rest of the group or class, according to the teacher's instructions.

1. Fill out the evaluation form.
2. Write two questions to ask the speaker after the presentation.
3. How did the speaker handle the question-and-answer session? Write down specific questions that might have been difficult to answer. How did the speaker respond to these questions?

4. Pay particular attention to the visual aids the speaker used. Consider the following questions in analyzing the strengths and weaknesses of the visual aids used by the speaker:
   A. Were the visual aids easy to see—simple and clear?
   B. Were the visual aids the right size—large enough to be seen by everyone?
   C. Did each visual aid focus on only one idea?
   D. Was the visual aid neatly prepared with as few words as possible?

5. Pay particular attention to the way the speaker used visual aids. Consider the following questions in analyzing the strengths and weaknesses of the way the speaker handled the visuals:
   A. Did the speaker face the audience when presenting the visual aids?
   B. Did the speaker use the right number of visual aids?
   C. Did the speaker explain the visual aid clearly?
   D. Did the visual aid support or emphasize an important point of the presentation?
   E. Did the speaker show the visual aid only when it was needed?
   F. Did the speaker follow the specific guidelines if he or she used the board, a flip chart, or an overhead projector?

Presentation Evaluation 5

Speaker: _____

Topic: _____

Evaluator: _____

Rating System
Complete the following evaluation form by filling in the appropriate number of points in the blanks provided. The point values are as follows:

2 = Excellent   1 = Satisfactory   0 = Needs Improvement

These points can be added up to give a total score for each section on the form. Follow your teacher's instructions in rating the speaker on one, some, or all of the sections included in this form. Space is provided on the form for your comments on specific strengths or weaknesses of the speaker's presentation. You can also add suggestions for improving future presentations.

I. *Delivery*

Points out of 10: _____   *Comments:*

_____ A. volume—loud enough
        to be heard clearly
_____ B. eye contact with audi-
        ence
_____ C. natural delivery—not
        read or memorized
_____ D. rate of speech—not too
        fast or too slow
_____ E. posture/body move-
        ment—no distracting
        mannerisms

II. *Content*

Points out of 10: _____   *Comments:*

_____ A. clear central idea
_____ B. topic suitable for time
available—not too limited
or too general
_____ C. topic suitable for this
audience—not too
technical or too
well-known
_____ D. topic developed with
relevant details, facts,
examples that provide
strong support of central
idea
_____ E. presentation meets time
requirements—not too
long or too short

III. *Organization*

Points out of 10: _____   *Comments:*

_____ A. introduction
_____ B. use of transitions
_____ C. main points clearly stated
_____ D. development of ideas
logical, easy to follow
_____ E. conclusion

IV. *Language*

Points out of 6: _____   *Comments:*

_____ A. accuracy of
communication—clarity
of ideas

_____ B. vocabulary appropriate
for this audience—
difficult or technical
words explained
_____ C. pronunciation/intonation

V. *Visual Aids*

Points out of 4: _____   *Comments:*

_____ A. easy to see—simple,
clear, right size
_____ B. helpful in clarifying
topic

Total Number of Points Received by Speaker: _____

Total Number of Possible Points: _____

Questions to ask the speaker:

1. _____

2. _____

Comparing

Expressions

The following list includes only some of the many possible expressions that are used to convey each function. Space is provided for you to add other expressions related to each function as you work through the unit. Before going over the lists provided, you may want to discuss each function and then work individually or in small groups to list expressions that you are already familiar with. You can identify any expressions that seem to be particularly formal, informal, direct, or indirect and then compare them with those listed here. You might also discuss possible situations in which these expressions could appropriately be used.

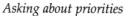

Asking about priorities

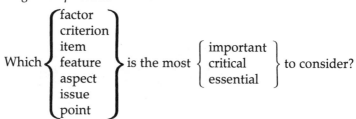

Which { factor / criterion / item / feature / aspect / issue / point } is the most { important / critical / essential } to consider?

Stating priorities

The most $\left\{\begin{array}{l}\text{important}\\\text{critical}\\\text{essential}\end{array}\right\}$ $\left\{\begin{array}{l}\text{factor}\\\text{criterion}\\\text{item}\\\text{feature}\\\text{aspect}\\\text{issue}\\\text{point}\end{array}\right\}$ [to consider] is _____.

Comparing two solutions

This solution is $\left\{\begin{array}{l}\text{better}\\\text{worse}\end{array}\right\}$ than that one.

This solution is more $\left\{\begin{array}{l}\text{practical}\\\text{effective}\\\text{useful}\\\text{beneficial}\\\text{economical}\end{array}\right\}$ than that one.

Comparing three or more solutions

This solution is the $\left\{\begin{array}{l}\text{best}\\\text{worst}\end{array}\right\}$ one of all.

This solution is the most $\left\{\begin{array}{l}\text{practical}\\\text{effective}\\\text{useful}\\\text{beneficial}\\\text{economical}\end{array}\right\}$ of all.

Expressing similarities

They're $\left\{\begin{array}{l}\text{both}\\\text{all}\end{array}\right\}$ about the same.

One idea is as $\left\{\begin{array}{l}\text{good}\\\text{practical}\\\text{effective}\\\text{useful}\\\text{beneficial}\\\text{economical}\end{array}\right\}$ as the other.

There's not much difference $\left\{\begin{array}{l}\text{between}\\\text{among}\end{array}\right\}$ them.

Listening Practice

The following exercises can be completed by listening to Unit 14 on the tape.

Section 1.   There is one discussion in this section dealing with nuclear reactors. The major danger in all nuclear reactors is that the core of nuclear fuel will overheat, melt into an uncontrollable mass, break through containment walls, and release radioactivity. In order to prevent these meltdowns, the fuel in nuclear reactors is always surrounded with circulating coolant—ordinary water in most commercial reactors. In the following discussion one scientist is explaining his suggestion that the Energy Department build a different type of nuclear reactor, one that uses inert helium gas as a coolant instead of water.

A.   Examine the chart. What information do you need to complete it? Now listen to Section 1 on the tape. Put a check [✓] in the correct space.

According to the speaker, which reactor:	Types of Reactors	
	Standard Water-Cooled Reactor	*Proposed Gas-Cooled Reactor*
1. is smaller	_____	✓
2. is safer	_____	✓
3. is more economical initially	_____	✓
4. requires more expensive safety systems	_____	✓
5. is more cost-effective in the long run	_____	✓
6. has lower electrical output	_____	✓

B.   Work with a partner, in a small group, or as a class to compare your charts. Do you have the same information?

C.   Work with a partner or in a small group to discuss the following: Which type of nuclear reactor would you recommend building? Why? How does nuclear energy compare to other types of energy? Are nuclear reactors worth the risk?

Section 2.   There is one discussion in this section. Two company executives are comparing various aspects of life in three cities where they might be transferred: New York City, Tokyo, or Paris.

A.   Before listening to the discussion, work individually, with a partner, or in a small group to answer the following questions comparing New York City, Tokyo, and Paris.

Which city do you think (or know) has:

1. the largest population: _____

2. the most expensive housing: _____

3. the cheapest gasoline: _____

4. the cleanest air: _____

5. the most available green space (public parks):

_____

6. the lowest crime rate: _____

B.   Work with a partner or in a small group to compare your answers.

C.   Examine the following chart. What information do you need to complete it? Now listen to Section 2 on the tape. Fill in the chart with the specific information that you hear. You may need to listen to the discussion more than once to obtain all the necessary figures. When discussing money, these people are referring to prices or costs in U.S. dollars.

	New York	Tokyo	Paris
Population	736,000	_____	_____
Average monthly rent for a three-bedroom apartment	_____	_____	_____
Price of gas per American gallon	_____	_____	_____
Pollution	_____	_____	_____
Public park space per head	_____	_____	_____
Murders per 100,000 people	_____	_____	_____
Robberies per 100,000 people	_____	_____	_____

D. Work with a partner, in a small group, or as a class to compare your charts. Do you have the same information?

E. Now look at Section A again to compare your ideas with the information you heard in the discussion. How many of these answers were correct? Use the information in the chart to make any necessary changes to your answers in Section A.

F. Work with a partner or in a small group to discuss the following: Which of these three cities would you prefer to live in? Why? What else do you know about these cities that might influence your decision?

Controlled Practice

Exercise 1. Use different expressions from the unit in discussing the illustrations on page 214.

> *Speaker A:* Ask Speaker B's opinion.
>
> *Speaker B:* Compare the different things.

Exercise 2. Compare the following things according to the criteria provided in parentheses. You can also add your own criteria to each item to make other comparisons.

1. a uranium atom, a hydrogen atom (large)
2. plastic, leather (durable)
3. ecology, physics, astronomy (interesting)
4. private health care, public health care (efficient)
5. algebra, trigonometry, calculus (easy)
6. a slide rule, an electronic calculator (practical)
7. a laser beam printer, a dot matrix printer (expensive)
8. driving to work, using public transportation (convenient)
9. participating in a group discussion, making a presentation (stressful)
10. swimming, jogging, playing tennis (enjoyable)
11. a diamond, glass (hard)
12. first class, business class, economy class (cheap)
13. computer-aided instruction, lectures, class discussion (effective)
14. courses in management, courses in literature (beneficial)
15. the problem of overpopulation, the threat of nuclear war (urgent)
16. a portable computer, a mainframe computer (powerful, light)
17. a Rolls Royce, a Honda Civic, a Cadillac (comfortable, economical)

18. nuclear power, solar power (reliable, safe)
19. French, Russian, Chinese, Greek (difficult, useful)
20. aluminum, iron (heavy, resistant to corrosion)

Exercise 3.   Compare the suggested solutions using some of the criteria discussed in this course: cost, time, side effects, feasibility, acceptability, effectiveness. You can also add your own solutions to the problem. Be sure to support your opinions with reasons, facts, and examples. Students can work on this exercise in pairs or small groups and then compare ideas.

> *Example:*   In my opinion [It seems to me, I believe, etc.] that the first solution is more _____ than the second one because _____.

General Interest

1. *Problem:*   The Ministry of Industry predicts a shortage of workers in high-tech production by the year 2000.
   Solution 1: The government should encourage students to study high-tech fields.
   Solution 2: The government can retrain people to enable them to work in high-tech production.

2. *Problem:*   Over 700 million people lack sufficient food to lead an active working life.
   Solution 1: Countries with a surplus should give wheat to these people.
   Solution 2: The government should store bumper crop harvests for bad years in the future.

3. *Problem:*   Piracy of computer software is costing companies millions of dollars.
   Solution 1: The government should forbid the sale of pirated software.
   Solution 2: Companies should design software to make it impossible to be copied.

Science

4. *Problem:*   Genetic engineers working for the government have found a way to produce a hormone that increases milk production by 20%. However, this country already has a milk surplus.
   Solution 1: The government should ban production of this hormone.

Solution 2: The government should allow production of this hormone to encourage technological innovations.

5. *Problem:* A new bacterial infection affecting orange trees has been identified in several groves. If the disease spreads it could destroy the region's entire crop.

Solution 1: Farmers can plant resistant trees.

Solution 2: Farmers can burn the infected trees.

Solution 3: Farmers can use antibiotics on the trees.

6. *Problem:* A country faces deforestation because people are cutting down trees for fuel.

Solution 1: The government can establish efficient fuel wood plantations.

Solution 2: The government can pass a law to stop people from cutting down trees.

Engineering

7. *Problem:* Citizens in rural areas face severe shortages of safe drinking water.

Solution 1: Villages can build tanks to catch rain water.

Solution 2: The government can send water trains.

Solution 3: The government can provide free handpumps to villages.

8. *Problem:* A country has a highway fatality rate that is twenty times greater than the worldwide average.

Solution 1: The government can expand the role of the traffic engineering department.

Solution 2: The government can improve public transportation.

Solution 3: The government can introduce mobile patrols to give first aid.

Health

9. *Problem:* Pharmacists say poor storage has affected the quality of some of their drugs.

Solution 1: Pharmacists can destroy all of these drugs.

Solution 2: Pharmacists can try to improve the storage of drugs.

10. *Problem:* Patients are complaining about the high cost of prescription drugs.

Solution 1: Doctors can prescribe generic pills rather than brand names.

Solution 2: Doctors can prescribe fewer drugs.

Housing
Expensive?   Noisy?   Comfortable?   Desirable?

1. a suburban house

2. a trailer home

3. a city apartment

Assembly Lines
Efficient?   Fast?   Safe?   Clean?   Economical?   Practical?

1. humans on an assembly line

2. Robots on an assembly line

Communication Concepts

INDIVIDUAL BLOCKING ROLES

People have certain needs that can be satisfied by being a member of a group. Although the main objective of a group is to reach a decision, members of the group may also have personal goals in mind. For example, members may want to feel important, to have some power, to impress people, or to make friends. The group must meet some of these needs in order to encourage members to be productive. Effective groups solve problems and make decisions, but at the same time they must give satisfaction to individual members.

There are times when group members are more concerned with satisfying personal needs than in working toward the goals of the group. For instance, a person might be more interested in getting personal attention than in working toward a solution to the problem under discussion. Thus, by trying to find individual satisfaction, a group member may block the progress of the group.

These individual roles can harm group functioning and lead to poor group decisions. If a member starts to slow the progress of the group by taking on a blocking role, the group members should do all they can to discourage such behavior. Sometimes it may help to talk over these problems after the discussion so that members can improve the quality of the next discussion. Here are some examples of individual blocking roles that members should not take on:

1. *Withdrawing*

   People who withdraw are physically present during the discussion, but they do not participate in the discussion unless other members force them to do so.

2. *Dominating*

   Dominators try to take over a discussion. They may talk a lot and try to monopolize the discussion. Also, dominators may try to push through their own ideas or suggestions.

3. *Being aggressive*

   Aggressors blame others for problems. They may also show anger against another member or against the group.

4. *Blocking communication*

   Blockers stop the group's progress by arguing too much on one point, talking about irrelevant points, or rejecting others' ideas without any consideration. Also, blockers may not listen to other members since they feel that they already know everything. They won't change their minds even if strong reasons are presented.

5. *Getting special attention*

Some members try to call special attention to themselves by talking loudly or by acting in an unusual manner.

6. *Joking*

Members may laugh or joke too much or in an inappropriate way. This stops serious work from getting done.

Discussion Techniques

RETURNING TO THE SUBJECT

In a good discussion a speaker's comments should be relevant both to the general subject and to the specific point under discussion. If a speaker says something that is not related to the subject at hand, it is usually the group leader's responsibility to point this out. Of course, it is extremely important to do this in a polite way without suddenly cutting that person off. Here are some comments to bring the discussion back to the subject:

> Yes, that's an interesting idea, but it raises a different point. Could we come back to it a bit later?

> That's a good idea. Let's come back to it later once we've finished discussing _____.

> I think that's a point worth discussing. However, let's see if anyone has anything to add here before we move on to a different subject.

> That's an interesting point, but perhaps it's a bit off the subject. We're discussing _____.

Discussion Practice

DETERMINING CRITERIA

The cases in this section are designed to give you practice in determining the best criteria to use in making a particular decision or evaluation. Criteria are standards that serve as a basis for making an evaluation, judgment, or decision. Look at the following examples of criteria developed for three different kinds of decisions:

1. Possible criteria to judge a student's individual performance in a group discussion:
   • interaction
   • use of expressions
   • content
   • accuracy
   (Of course, other criteria, such as attitude or fluency, could be substituted or added to the four listed here.)
2. Possible criteria to judge solutions to a problem of low production:
   • cost
   • time
   • feasibility
   • acceptability
3. Possible criteria to use in deciding which assembly line worker to promote to supervisor:
   • seniority
   • productivity record
   • recommendations from other supervisors
   • education
   • intelligence
   • leadership skills in informal activities

After you have developed a list of possible criteria, you can decide which criteria are the most important to use in making that particular decision. Then in the decision-making process the group members can evaluate each solution (item, location, or person) according to how well each one meets the established criteria.

Instructions

1. Work in small groups. All groups may be assigned to work on the same case(s) in order to compare results, or groups may work on different cases according to their particular interests.
2. Choose a group leader. Work together to brainstorm possible criteria to use in making the decision. One group member should make a list of these ideas on a separate sheet of paper.
3. After considering all the ideas developed during the brainstorming session, work together to agree on the three most important criteria. These criteria do not have to be ranked in order of importance.

4. Work individually to fill in the worksheet(s) according to your group's decision.
5. If other groups have worked on the same case(s), compare results.
6. After you have finished, complete the Participant Evaluation Form on page 221.

Worksheets

Criteria to Use in Case # _____.

1. _____
2. _____
3. _____

Criteria to Use in Case # _____.

1. _____
2. _____
3. _____

Criteria to Use in Case # _____.

1. _____
2. _____
3. _____

Of course, you will have to develop specific criteria to fit each particular situation. However, the following points may help you think of possible criteria to use:

age	experience	quality
attitude	fairness	reliability
convenience	honesty	reputation
cost	location	safety
creativity	organization	service
economy	performance	size
education	personality	speed
efficiency	practicality	time

CASE 1: THE BEST ASSIGNMENT

Situation

What criteria should you use in judging the best written report for one assignment in a technical writing course?

CASE 2: THE BEST JOB APPLICANT

Situation

What criteria should you use in selecting the best job applicant to hire as a research scientist?

CASE 3: THE BEST UNIVERSITY

Situation

What criteria should you use in selecting the best university for advanced study in your field?

CASE 4: THE BEST DENTIST

Situation

What criteria should you use in choosing the best dentist for your family?

CASE 5: THE BEST ZOO

Situation

What criteria should you use in judging the best zoo in the world?

CASE 6: THE BEST COMPUTER

Situation

What criteria should you use in selecting the best computer for a small office?

CASE 7: THE BEST CAR

Situation

What criteria should you use in deciding which make of car to buy for company executives?

CASE 8: THE BEST LOCATION

Situation

What criteria should you use in selecting the best place to locate another factory?

Discussion Evaluation

PARTICIPANT EVALUATION FORM

1. Identifying the group

   A. Discussion topic: _____

   B. Names of other students in your group: _____

   _____

2. Did all group members take an active part in reaching the final decision?

   _____

3. Did you have trouble agreeing on the criteria? How were conflicts resolved?

   _____

   _____

4. Did any particular group member(s) influence the final decision? How or why did they have this effect?

   _____

   _____

5. How long did it take to reach a final decision?

   _____

6. How was the leader chosen?

   _____ A. general agreement

   _____ B. voting

   _____ C. someone volunteered

   _____ D. the instructor appointed someone

   _____ E. _____

7. Do you think that this was the best way to choose a leader? Why or why not?

   _____

   _____

   _____

8. How did the group reach a decision?

_____ A. *Consensus.* The group reached a general agreement.

_____ B. *Majority rule.* The group chose the item(s) that more than half the group agreed on.

_____ C. *Voting.* Since there was no clear majority for an item, the members voted and those items with the most votes won.

_____ D. *Authority.* The leader or a strong participant pushed through a decision.

_____ E. *Default.* The group could not reach a decision.

_____ F. *Other.* _____

9. How do you think your group could have improved the decision-making process?

_____

_____

_____

Group Discussion Skills

Persuading

Expressions

The following list includes only some of the many possible expressions that are used to convey each function. Space is provided for you to add other expressions related to each function as you work through the unit. Before going over the lists provided, you may want to discuss each function and then work individually or in small groups to list expressions that you are already familiar with. You can identify any expressions that seem to be particularly formal, informal, direct, or indirect and then compare them with those listed here. You might also discuss possible situations in which these expressions could appropriately be used.

Persuading
You must admit that _____.
You have to agree that _____.
Don't forget that _____.
Let's not forget that _____.

Don't you $\begin{Bmatrix} \text{agree} \\ \text{think} \end{Bmatrix}$ that _____?

Counterarguing
Even so, _____.
But still, _____.
Still, _____.
Nevertheless, _____.

But then again, _____.
All the same, _____.
In any case, _____.
Anyway, _____.

Even if that is $\begin{Bmatrix} \text{true,} \\ \text{so,} \end{Bmatrix}$ _____.

Conceding
   Yes, I'll go along with that.
   I'll agree with you there.
   I'm willing to go along with you.
   In that case, _____.
   Well, you've convinced me.

Listening Practice

The following exercises can be completed by listening to Unit 15 on the tape.

Section 1.   There is one discussion in this section. Three people are discussing the possibility of irradiating fresh meats, fruits, and vegetables.

A.   What are some of the arguments for and against the irradiation of food? Before listening to the discussion, work individually, with a partner, or in a small group to brainstorm arguments for and against this action. List your ideas in the chart.

Irradiating Food

Arguments for	*Arguments against*

B. Now listen to Section 1 on the tape. Put a check next to the arguments you hear that are the same as the ones you have written. Then add any other arguments that the speakers use.

C. Listen again. Which expressions do the speakers use for persuading and counterarguing? Write the expressions in the order that you hear them. Identify the expressions as persuading (P) or counterarguing (C) in the blank in front of each number.

P or C   *Expressions*

_____ 1. _____

_____ 2. _____

_____ 3. _____

_____ 4. _____

_____ 5. _____

_____ 6. _____

_____ 7. _____

_____ 8. _____

_____ 9. _____

D. Work with a partner, in a small group, or as a class to compare the expressions you have listed.

Section 2. There is one discussion in this section. Company executives are discussing the possibility that their company will move from its present location in a large capital city to a small city about 200 kilometers away.

A. What are some arguments for and against moving a company from a large capital city to a smaller city in the same country? Before listening to the discussion, work individually, with a partner, or in a small group to brainstorm arguments for and against this move. List your ideas in the chart.

Moving to a Smaller City

Arguments for	*Arguments against*

B. Now listen to Section 2 on the tape. Put a check next to the arguments you hear that are the same as the ones you have written. Then add any other arguments that the speakers use.

C. Listen again. Which expressions do the speakers use for persuading and counterarguing? Write the expressions in the order that you hear them. Identify the expressions as persuading (P) or counterarguing (C) in the blank in front of each number.

P or C   *Expressions*

_____ 1. _____

_____ 2. _____

_____ 3. _____

_____ 4. _____

_____ 5. _____

_____ 6. _____

_____ 7. _____

_____ 8. _____

D. Work with a partner, in a small group, or as a class to compare the expressions you have listed.

Controlled Practice

Exercise 1. Look at the photographs on page 228. These photographs show situations that require urgent action. What action do you think should be taken immediately to solve the problem or to improve the situation? Use a variety of expressions from the unit in discussing these photographs.

Speaker A: Explain the situation and persuade Speaker B that a particular action must be taken immediately.

Speaker B: Counterargue.

Exercise 2.   Use a variety of expressions from the unit.

Student A: Tell Student B what you intend to do.

Student B: Try to persuade Student B *not* to take that action.

Student A: Counterargue.

Student B: Try again to persuade Student A.

Student A: Counterargue or concede.

General Interest

1. start smoking again
2. go bird hunting
3. sign a petition against nuclear energy
4. stop attending this class
5. buy an ivory carving
6. not donate blood during a hospital blood drive
7. take sleeping pills
8. learn to fly a glider
9. stop your daily exercise
10. not wear seat belts

Science

11. spray your vegetable garden with DDT
12. buy a 2-cylinder car
13. watch an eclipse of the sun while wearing sunglasses
14. work for a company that produces asbestos
15. put out poison to kill mice in your house

Engineering

16. not spend money on insulating your new house
17. disconnect the catalytic converter on your car
18. build an apartment building on the San Andreas Fault
19. build a windmill to provide energy for your home
20. not put down carpeting in a concert auditorium

We Have to Take Action Immediately!

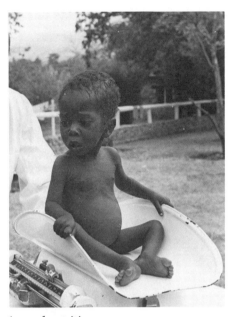

1. malnutrition

2. pollution

3. traffic

4. overpopulation

Health

21. go to the dentist only when you have a toothache
22. try cocaine
23. take penicillin to help you get over a cold
24. take double the prescribed dose of medicine
25. not sign an organ donation card

Exercise 3. Use a variety of expressions from the unit.

> *Student A:* Give an opinion.
>
> *Student B:* Try to persuade Student A to change his or her mind.
>
> *Student A:* Counterargue.
>
> *Student B:* Try again to persuade Student A.
>
> *Student A:* Counterargue or concede.

General Interest

1. The government should [should not] provide free health care.
2. Resources should [should not] be spent on preventative health measures rather than on high-technology medicine.
3. The government should [should not] allow lead in gasoline.
4. The government should [should not] allow the sale of cigarettes.
5. Spent radioactive waste should [should not] be shipped through densely populated areas.
6. All university students should [should not] be required to take a minimum number of university-level science courses.
7. The government should [should not] require automobile drivers and passengers to wear seatbelts.
8. A postgraduate degree is [is not] inferior to on-the-job experience.
9. The government should [should not] prevent companies from introducing new packaging that will create litter.
10. Most people want [do not want] to work as a team.

Science

11. Research into new biological warfare agents should [should not] be banned.
12. Studying animals in the wild is [is not] better than studying them in the laboratory.
13. Low-level doses of antibiotics should [should not] be added to animal feeds.
14. Chemical pesticides are [are not] the best way to eliminate mosquitoes that spread disease.

15. The lives of most people have [have not] been affected by genetic engineering.

Engineering

16. Rubbish should [should not] be used as landfill.
17. The government should [should not] inspect cars annually.
18. The storage of high-level radioactive waste should [should not] be centralized.
19. Humans are [are not] better than robots on the assembly line.
20. Hard water should [should not] be softened by adding chemicals to remove the calcium salts.

Health

21. The government should [should not] allow nurses to strike.
22. Fluoride should [should not] be taken as a dietary supplement.
23. Sleeping pills are [are not] beneficial for people who suffer from insomnia.
24. The government should [should not] pay for cosmetic surgery.
25. The government should [should not] make AIDS testing compulsory for everyone in the nation.

Communication Concepts

NONVERBAL COMMUNICATION

Nonverbal communication involves sending messages without using words. Think, for example, how people can communicate the following feelings and ideas without saying a single word:

"Yes."	"I'd like to say something."
"No."	"This is boring."
"I don't know."	"Calm down."
"Wait a minute."	"I feel impatient."

These messages are communicated through the use of eye contact, facial expressions, gestures, and body posture.

Nonverbal communication can actually express more than verbal communication. However, these nonverbal messages are not always the same in different cultures. For instance, eye contact can be interpreted in various ways. In some cultures speakers are expected to look directly at the listeners, while in other cultures it is a sign of disrespect to look somebody directly in the eye. For speakers participating in meetings with English speakers, it is important to understand how they use these nonverbal messages. Here are some examples:

Eye Contact

1. Speakers who look directly at group members seem more self-confident and sure of themselves. Thus, group members are more likely to be persuaded by a speaker who maintains eye contact with them.
2. When listeners look at the speaker, they show that they are listening. By showing that they are paying attention, listeners encourage speakers to express their ideas.
3. One way people can show they are willing to speak is to look directly at the group leader.
4. If speakers do not want to speak or participate in the discussion, they usually do not establish eye contact with the group leader.
5. Group members may be able to quiet someone who is talking too much by avoiding eye contact.
6. It is possible for the group leader to bring members into the discussion just by looking directly at them.

Facial Expressions

7. Group members can encourage a speaker to continue by smiling or nodding their heads.
8. By frowning or raising an eyebrow, listeners can let the speaker know that they don't understand the message or that they disagree.

Body Posture

9. By leaning forward, a person can show agreement or interest and thus encourage a speaker.
10. By leaning forward, a person can also show his or her intention to speak.
11. By leaning backward, a person can show disagreement or lack of interest and thus discourage the speaker.
12. A person with folded arms may look closed to the discussion. This can discourage interaction.

Gestures

13. Group members can request permission to speak by raising a hand or a finger. In informal groups, however, members do not usually raise their hands before speaking.

14. If someone is trying to interrupt, the speaker may put out his or her hand. This is a signal that the person should allow the speaker to finish talking.

What other messages can you think of that can be sent nonverbally? Can you think of ways these messages may change from culture to culture?

Discussion Techniques

SUMMARIZING

At certain points in the discussion it is useful for the leader to summarize what has happened so far. This is often done to test for consensus—to see whether the members are ready to agree on a particular point. Also, a leader often summarizes what has been decided so far before going on to another point. Some possible expressions to use in summarizing are:

Let's summarize what we've $\begin{Bmatrix} \text{decided} \\ \text{agreed on} \end{Bmatrix}$ so far.

Do we agree that _____?
Then we agree that _____?

So far, we've $\begin{Bmatrix} \text{decided} \\ \text{agreed} \end{Bmatrix}$ that _____.

In addition, the leader usually summarizes final conclusions the group has reached at the end of the discussion:

In $\begin{Bmatrix} \text{conclusion,} \\ \text{summary,} \end{Bmatrix}$ _____.

To $\begin{Bmatrix} \text{summarize,} \\ \text{conclude,} \end{Bmatrix}$ _____.

Discussion Practice

SOLVING A PROBLEM

The cases in this section will give you further practice in participating in problem-solving discussions.

Instructions

1. Refer to the detailed instructions included in the Discussion Practice section of Unit 2 for guidance in choosing cases, getting organized, brainstorming, selecting ideas, and preparing for and starting the discussion. In your discussion the group leader should try to keep the group moving toward the goal in an organized way.
2. After participating in the discussion, all group members can complete the Participant Self-Evaluation Form on page 237. Group observers should complete the Observer Evaluation Form on page 238 as directed by the instructor. They can then discuss their evaluations with the group members. If other groups have worked on the same case, compare your solutions.

CASE 1: ERUPTION PREDICTED

Situation

A volcano near a heavily populated area has begun to spout ash. Some geologists have predicted that a major eruption will follow within weeks. If people are in the area when the volcano erupts, the consequences will be disastrous. Therefore, they want the government authorities to evacuate more than 100,000 residents immediately. Residents, however, are aware that predicting eruptions is an imprecise science. Although the volcano might erupt in a few weeks, it could be months before an actual eruption. In fact, it is not certain whether an eruption will ever occur. Residents oppose evacuation because they do not want to disrupt their lives over something that may never happen. Furthermore, an evacuation would cost the community millions of dollars. A meeting has been called to discuss the situation.

Purpose of the Discussion

Group members should try to agree on the best way to deal with the possible volcanic eruption in this area.

Group Roles

The following people take part in the discussion:

> Leader: a representative of the government
> Geologist(s)
> Resident(s)

CASE 2: SCIENTISTS AS POLICY MAKERS

Situation

The government in a developed country plans to build three new nuclear power stations. The government's plan rejects the recommendations of scientific experts. These experts were asked by the government to examine the use of nuclear power in the country's energy program. After an in-depth study, the scientists recommended that no more nuclear power stations be built. Instead they proposed a program that would conserve energy and increase the use of renewable energy sources, such as solar energy and hydroelectric power. The scientific community has questioned the government's decision. Scientists believe that government policies should follow the recommendations of specialists in the field. The National Association for the Development of Science and Technology has called a meeting to discuss the issue.

Purpose of the Discussion

Group members should try to agree on the best way to strengthen the role of scientists in making policy decisions.

Group Roles

The following people take part in the discussion:

> Leader: a representative of the National Association for the
> Development of Science and Technology
> Scientist(s)
> Government representative(s)

CASE 3: TOXIC WASTE

Situation

Residents of a new housing development claim that they have higher-than-normal rates of miscarriages and of blood and liver abnormalities. Investigations have revealed that the housing development is built on a chemical waste landfill. The chemicals have been leaking into the soil and water. Residents say the chemical company that created the landfill is responsible for their health problems. They have demanded that the company take immediate action. The company says that independent studies have shown absolutely no causal relationship between the chemicals in the fill and the residents' health. Therefore, they refuse to accept any liability. Residents have asked the government to do something about this problem. A meeting has been called to discuss the situation.

Purpose of the Discussion

Group members should try to agree on the best way to deal with this landfill problem.

Group Roles

The following people take part in the discussion:

> Leader: a representative of the government
> Representative(s) of the chemical company
> Resident(s)

CASE 4: HEART TRANSPLANTATION

Situation

Hospital administrators have recommended to the Chief of Medical Service that the hospital should stop performing heart transplants. The administrators say that heart transplantation uses costly and scarce resources for a procedure that benefits very few patients. At the same time, because of limited resources, the hospital is forced to deny services to many patients who need help. Administrators believe that medical procedures should be evaluated in terms of the greatest good for the greatest number. Several cardiologists disagree. They maintain that important scientific advances might unexpectedly result from transplant operations. Furthermore, they argue that it is unfair to deny their patients a procedure that could prolong their lives. A meeting has been called to discuss the issue.

Purpose of the Discussion

Group members should try to agree on the best policy for the hospital to adopt regarding heart transplantation.

Group Roles

The following people take part in the discussion:

> Leader: the Chief of Medical Service
> Hospital administrator(s)
> Cardiologist(s)
> Representative(s) of patients needing heart transplants

Discussion Evaluation

A. PARTICIPANT SELF-EVALUATION FORM

After you participate in a group discussion, complete the following form:

1. *Rating your own performance.* Use the following scales to rate your own performance:

    A. *Interaction.* Did you effectively interact with others? Use a variety of functions? Initiate? Involve others? Ask questions?

Excellent	Satisfactory	Weak	Unsatisfactory
3	2	1	0

    B. *Use of Expressions.* Did you effectively and accurately use a variety of expressions?

Excellent	Satisfactory	Weak	Unsatisfactory
3	2	1	0

    C. *Content.* Did you contribute logical, relevant information and ideas? Stay on the subject? Analyze solutions? Show strong support of arguments?

Excellent	Satisfactory	Weak	Unsatisfactory
3	2	1	0

    D. *Accuracy.* Did you communicate ideas clearly with effective control of grammar, vocabulary, and pronunciation?

Excellent	Satisfactory	Weak	Unsatisfactory
3	2	1	0

2. *Improvement.* Answer the following questions:

A. How do you think you have improved your speaking skills since the beginning of the course?

_____

_____

_____

B. Which activities do you think have helped you to improve the most?

_____

_____

_____

_____

B. OBSERVER EVALUATION FORM

1. *Identifying the group*

A. Discussion topic: _____

B. Names of students in group: _____

_____

2. *Listening to the discussion.* Look at the rating scales listed in #3. Use a separate sheet of paper to take notes on the group discussion in order to be able to rate the group according to these criteria.

3. *Rating the discussion.* Use the following scales to rate the discussion group:

A. *Participation.* Did all group members interact and take equal part in the discussion?

Excellent	Satisfactory	Weak	Unsatisfactory
3	2	1	0

____|_____|_____|_____|____

B. *Clarity*. Did all group members speak loudly and clearly?

Excellent	Satisfactory	Weak	Unsatisfactory
3	2	1	0

C. *Pace.* Did the discussion move along at the right speed, without long pauses between speakers?

Excellent	Satisfactory	Weak	Unsatisfactory
3	2	1	0

D. *Problem Solving.* Did the discussion move in an organized, logical way toward the final decision?

Excellent	Satisfactory	Weak	Unsatisfactory
3	2	1	0

E. *Leader Control.* Did the leader effectively guide the discussion, not taking too much or too little control?

Excellent	Satisfactory	Weak	Unsatisfactory
3	2	1	0

Appendices

Appendix I

PRESENTATION WORKSHEETS

Student Worksheet 1. Brainstorming Subjects for Class Presentations

Name: _____

Brainstorm possible subjects for your class presentations by filling in the chart on pages 242 and 243. Do not try to work out specific topics or titles of reports right now. Simply write down words or ideas in each category as they come to mind.

Work/research   *Studies*

Interests/hobbies *Current issues*

Sample Worksheet 1. Brainstorming Subjects for Class Presentations

Work/research	*Studies*
WHO	immunology
epidemics	environment
health care in Africa	ecology
viruses	health
mercury poisoning	
preventive medicine	

Interests/hobbies	Current issues
travel	solar power
foreign countries	developing countries
computers	war
reading	child labor
hiking	energy crisis
fitness	poverty
conservation	education
	world hunger
	public health care
	toxic waste
	women's issues
	minority rights
	crime

Student Worksheet 2. Analyzing the Audience

Name: _____

1. Who are your listeners?

   Common occupation: _____

   Position in company: _____

   General level of education: _____

   Area of specialization: _____

   Special interests in common: _____

   Other important factors: _____

2. What is the general level of English of your listeners?

   Most of the listeners are:

   A. native speakers

   B. native and non-native speakers—mixed

   C. non-native speakers—generally advanced level

   D. non-native speakers—generally intermediate level

   E. non-native speakers at different levels

3. How much technical background do the listeners have?

   Most of the listeners are:

   A. experts in the field

   B. technically informed

   C. nontechnical

   D. mixed technical backgrounds

   E. don't know

4. How much do the listeners already know about the subject?

   _____

5. What do the listeners expect from your presentation?

   A. What do the listeners want or need to know?

   _____

B. When is the presentation due?

_____

C. How long should the presentation be?

_____

D. Are there any special guidelines? If so, what are they?

_____

6. What other details of the speaking situation might affect your presentation?

A. How many people will be in the audience?

_____

B. How will the listeners be seated—in rows, in a circle, around a table, or in another way?

_____

C. Will you be expected to stand in front of the listeners, sit in front of them, sit at a large table with them, or what?

_____

D. Will the situation be formal or informal?

_____

E. Where will the presentation be given? How large will the room be?

_____

F. What facilities will be available that you need to use?

_____

Sample Worksheet 2. Analyzing the Audience

1. Who are your listeners?

Common occupation: _professionals in science/English students_

Position in company: _high level_

General level of education: _university graduates_

Area of specialization: _many different areas_

Special interests in common: _scientific / technical issues_

Other important factors: _many different nationalities_

2. What is the general level of English of your listeners?

Most of the listeners are:

A. native speakers

B. native and non-native speakers—mixed

C. non-native speakers—generally advanced level

D. non-native speakers—generally intermediate level

(E.) non-native speakers at different levels

3. How much technical background do the listeners have?

Most of the listeners are:

A. experts in the field

(B.) technically informed

C. nontechnical

D. mixed technical backgrounds

E. don't know

4. How much do the listeners already know about the subject?

not much about my specialty – health

5. What do the listeners expect from your presentation?

A. What do the listeners want or need to know?

They want to know about current health issues.

B. When is the presentation due?

in a week, on March 1

C. How long should the presentation be?

5 - 7 minutes

D. Are there any special guidelines? If so, what are they?

follow guidelines in text – DO NOT READ NOTES!

6. What other details of the speaking situation might affect your presentation?

    A. How many people will be in the audience?

       about 20

    B. How will the listeners be seated—in rows, in a circle, around a table, or in another way?

       in rows

    C. Will you be expected to stand in front of the listeners, sit in front of them, sit at a large table with them, or what?

       stand in front of them

    D. Will the situation be formal or informal?

       informal

    E. Where will the presentation be given? How large will the room be?

       in the classroom

    F. What facilities will be available that you need to use?

       blackboard + chalk always available

Student Worksheet 3. Selecting Possible Topics

Name: _____

Possible topics for a class presentation:

1. _____

2. _____

3. _____

Sample Worksheet 3. Selecting Possible Topics

Possible topics for a class presentation:

1. *setting up local health clinics in Asia*
2. *primary health care*
3. *reasons that baby formula should not be used*

Student Worksheet 4. Organizing the Presentation

Name: _____

Topic: _____

Central idea: _____

Pattern of organization: _____

Sample Worksheet 4. Organizing the Presentation

Topic: *primary health care* _____

Central idea: *to describe the basic elements of primary health care*

Pattern of organization: *topical* _____

Student Worksheet 5. Writing a Planning Outline

You should write a planning outline to organize all of the information that you want to present in your presentation. You can use the following outline form as a guide in preparing your own outline. Of course, you can make changes in this outline according to the number of main points and details that you want to discuss.

Name: _____

Topic: _____

Central idea: _____

Pattern of organization: _____

INTRODUCTION

   I. Main point: _____

      A. _____

      B. _____

  II. Main point: _____

      A. _____

      B. _____

BODY

  I. Main point: _____

     A._____

     B. _____

     C._____

     D._____

 II. Main point: _____

     A._____

     B. _____

     C._____

     D._____

III. Main point: _____

     A._____

     B. _____

     C._____

     D._____

IV. Main point: _____

     A._____

     B. _____

     C._____

     D._____

CONCLUSION

  I. Main point: _____

     A._____

     B. _____

 II. Main point: _____

Sample Worksheet 5. Writing a Planning Outline

Topic: Primary Health Care

Central idea: Basic elements of primary health care

Pattern of organization: Topical

INTRODUCTION

I. Problem

   A. Millions of children in developing countries die each year from preventable diseases.

   B. The main killers in developing countries are diseases that are no longer a problem in rich countries, such as measles, polio, tuberculosis.

II. Past history

   A. In the 1970s the World Health Organization (WHO) tried to improve health care in developing countries by spending money on drugs, pesticides, and central hospitals in cities.

   B. Since these high-technology cures were not effective, in 1978 WHO began to work on prevention—stopping diseases before they start.

III. New program

   A. WHO developed a program called "primary health care" to help children and child-bearing women—those hardest hit by disease.

   B. This primary health care has five basic elements.

BODY

I. Clean water

   A. In the third world, 80% of infections are spread by water.

   B. WHO wants to provide all developing countries with clean water and good sanitation.

   C. This is the most expensive part of the program.

II. Immunization

   A. WHO wants to immunize children against common infections such as polio, measles, and tuberculosis.

B. WHO wants to make immunization available to every new-born baby.

C. This program is cheap—about $5 per child.

III. Education of mothers

A. WHO believes that lowering the birth rate can help solve health problems.

B. WHO encourages contraception and gives advice on birth control.

C. Up to 25% of maternal deaths during childbirth could be eliminated by simple improvements in hygiene, such as using sterile equipment.

D. Mothers can be trained to treat diarrhea in children—a major killer—by using simple and cheap means.

IV. Medical training

A. WHO wants more training for local health workers chosen by villagers.

B. This will help people in rural areas.

V. Essential drugs

A. Most third-world countries buy drugs from western companies—a waste of money.

B. Most poor countries are short of necessary drugs to treat common diseases or injuries.

C. WHO has a list of 220 essential drugs.

D. WHO can buy these drugs in large quantities (often at half price) to give to developing countries.

CONCLUSION

I. Primary health care is a practical, effective plan to improve health care.

II. WHO wants to achieve health care for all by the year 2000.

III. This is possible if countries give primary health care a high priority.

Worksheet 6. Making Your Presentation Notes

Use small index or note cards to outline the main ideas you want to present in your presentation. These notes should be made up of key words and short phrases to help you remember the important points. You can refer to these brief notes (not to your planning outline) during your report. Here is an example of some presentation notes:

[Intro]   ①

    Write on board : prevention

                    sanitation

                    immunization

                    contraception

Briefly explain meanings.

[Intro cont.]   ②

1. Millions of children in developing countries
   die each year — preventable diseases
2. Main killers no longer a problem in
   developing countries
3. WHO - 1970's — high tech — not work
4. 1978 — primary health care plan

---

③

[Body]

1. Clean water
   - 80% infections spread by H_2O
   - expensive program

2. Immunization
   - protect children against common illnesses
   - cheap program

④

3. Education of mothers
   - WHO believes in lowering birth rate
   - gives advice on contraception
   - simple hygiene can stop 25% maternal deaths
   - mothers can be trained to fight diarrhea

---

⑤

4. Medical training
   - train local health workers
   - help rural areas
5. Essential drugs
   - WHO has list of 220 essential drugs
   - can buy in large quantity at
     $\frac{1}{2}$ price

---

⑥

[Conclusion]

1. Primary health care — practical
2. Health care for all by the year 2000
3. Priority

Appendix II

FINAL CHECKLIST FOR PREPARING AN ORAL PRESENTATION

Effective speakers generally follow these steps when preparing an oral presentation.

1. Determining your topic
   A. Choose a subject.
   B. Analyze your listeners (Worksheet 2).
   C. Select possible topics for your presentation based on the analysis of your listeners (Worksheet 3).
   D. Choose your final topic with the instructor's approval.
   E. Write a clear statement of the central idea of your presentation and select the pattern of organization that best suits your topic (Worksheet 4).

2. Collecting data
   A. Based on what you already know about your subject, list the main points that your presentation will probably cover.
   B. Develop a working outline by putting these points in logical order.
   C. Use your working outline as a guide to collect all of the information you need.
   D. Do any necessary research. Use one note card for each idea. Keep track of your sources of information.

3. Organizing your information
   A. As you collect information, make necessary changes in your working outline. You may change, add, or drop main points as you learn more about your topic.
   B. Follow the introduction—body—conclusion form of organization.
   C. Start with the body of your presentation. Put all of the note cards related to each main point in separate groups.
   D. Work on one point at a time. Take all of the note cards on that subtopic and decide what to include and what to leave out of your presentation. Put the note cards in logical order.
   E. After you have developed all of the main points of your presentation, decide what, if any, visual aids you want to use.
   F. Plan the introduction and conclusion.
   G. Use your working outline and your note cards to write a detailed planning outline of everything you want to include in the presentation (Worksheet 5).

4. Final planning
    A. Review your planning outline until you know the material very well.
    B. Use your planning outline to write brief presentation notes on note cards (Worksheet 6).
    C. Prepare a list of any technical or specialized terms that you need to explain to the listeners. You may want to write these words on the board at the beginning of your presentation.
    D. Check with the instructor or a dictionary on the pronunciation of any new or unfamiliar vocabulary words.
    E. Practice giving your presentation, making sure that it meets the time requirements.

Appendix III

RATING SCALES WITH CRITERIA FOR EVALUATING INDIVIDUALS IN A GROUP DISCUSSION

Observers can use the following rating scales to evaluate individuals who are participating in a group discussion:

A. *Interaction.* Did the speaker effectively interact with others? Use a variety of functions? Initiate? Involve others? Ask questions?

Excellent	Satisfactory	Weak	Unsatisfactory
3	2	1	0

3: Effective interaction: uses a wide variety of functions; initiates; involves others; asks questions
2: Consistent interaction: may rely on a limited number of functions such as giving opinions, making statements, agreeing; takes some initiative; takes turns in speaking
1: Passive interaction: responds only by answering questions or tries to dominate/monopolize discussion
0: Lack of interaction: fails to participate or blocks group communication

B. *Use of Expressions.* Did the speaker effectively and accurately use a variety of expressions?

Excellent	Satisfactory	Weak	Unsatisfactory
3	2	1	0

3: Effective and accurate use of a wide variety of expressions

2: Appropriate and usually accurate use of different expressions

1: Inappropriate or inaccurate use of some expressions or repeated use of only two or three expressions

0: Failure to use any expressions or inappropriate or inaccurate use of many expressions

C. *Content.* Did the speaker contribute logical, relevant information and ideas? Stay on the subject? Analyze solutions? Show strong support of arguments?

Excellent	Satisfactory	Weak	Unsatisfactory
3	2	1	0

3: Contributes logical, relevant information and ideas; stays on the subject; analyzes solutions; strong support of arguments

2: Contributes ideas that relate to subject; makes some attempt to analyze solutions; limited support of arguments

1: Contributes few ideas to the discussion; may inappropriately change subject or make some irrelevant contributions; opinions lack support

0: Makes no meaningful contributions to discussion

D. *Accuracy.* Did the speaker communicate ideas clearly with effective control of grammar, vocabulary, and pronunciation?

Excellent	Satisfactory	Weak	Unsatisfactory
3	2	1	0

3: Precise communication: effective control of grammar/vocabulary/pronunciation, even with a few errors

2: Clear communication: a number of noticeable errors in grammar/vocabulary/pronunciation do not interfere with message

1: Faulty communication: frequent errors in grammar/vocabulary/pronunciation at times interfere with message; or insufficient number of utterances to judge accuracy

0: Lack of communication: serious errors block communication

Appendix IV

FORM FOR EVALUATING INDIVIDUALS IN A GROUP DISCUSSION

Name			
Role			
Total Points			
Interaction			
Use of Expressions			
Content			
Accuracy			

Name			
Role			
Total Points			
Interaction			
Use of Expressions			
Content			
Accuracy			

Appendix V

RATING SCALES FOR EVALUATING A GROUP DISCUSSION

Observer: _____

Topic: _____

Participants: _____

You can use the following rating scales to evaluate a group's performance after a group discussion.

A. *Participation.* Did all group members interact and take equal part
in the discussion?

Excellent	Satisfactory	Weak	Unsatisfactory
3	2	1	0

B. *Clarity.* Did all group members speak loudly and clearly?

Excellent	Satisfactory	Weak	Unsatisfactory
3	2	1	0

C. *Pace.* Did the discussion move along at the right speed, without
long pauses between speakers?

Excellent	Satisfactory	Weak	Unsatisfactory
3	2	1	0

D. *Problem Solving.* Did the discussion move in an organized, logical
way toward the final decision?

Excellent	Satisfactory	Weak	Unsatisfactory
3	2	1	0

E. *Leader Control.* Did the leader effectively guide the discussion, not
taking too much or too little control?

Excellent	Satisfactory	Weak	Unsatisfactory
3	2	1	0

Appendix VI

GUIDELINES FOR DEVELOPING CASES FOR DISCUSSION

In order to provide a variety of problem-solving role plays that are of interest to a particular class, the instructor and students may wish to develop their own cases for discussion. Students may work individually, in pairs, or small groups to write cases to use in addition to or in place of the cases included in the text. These guidelines will help students develop cases to discuss in problem-solving role plays:

1. Choose a problem in class, at work, in the community, or in the country where you live. You can often find good ideas in newspapers or magazines.
2. Write a brief explanation of the problem in one paragraph. Be sure that the conflict is clearly stated.
3. Decide on the different roles that should be represented in the discussion.
4. Write out the case following the format used in this text: (1) situation, (2) purpose of the discussion, and (3) group roles.
5. Put a title on the case you have developed and turn it in to the instructor. Be sure to include your name(s) on this paper.
6. Work with the instructor to make any necessary changes in the case.
7. The instructor will assign the case to your group or perhaps to another group to discuss in a problem-solving role play. Pay attention as the topic is discussed in class. Decide whether you need to make any changes. Can you improve the explanation of the situation? Is more information needed, or is there some information that could be left out? Is the purpose of the discussion clear? Should any of the roles be changed?
8. Hand in the final copy of your case to the instructor.